BREAKING CHAINS AGAINST ALL ODDS

BREAKING CHAINS AGAINST ALL ODDS

How God Rescued Me from 20 Years of Sex Trafficking

BREAKING CHAINS AGAINST ALL ODDS
How God Rescued Me from 20 Years of Sex Trafficking

By Jean Davis
WITH DAVE FICERE

Edited by Dave Ficere
Cover Design and Typesetting by Yvonne Parks at PearCreative.ca

Published by:

adamcolwellwriteworks.com

Printed in the United States of America

Print ISBN: 979-8-9885033-0-9
eBook ISBN: 979-8-9885033-1-6

DEDICATION

I dedicate this book to my two children,
whom I love with all my heart.

Thank you to my Lord and Savior, Jesus Christ,
for saving my life and setting me free.

A special thank you to Phyllis Phelps for being willing to share Jesus Christ with me and the many other women you have helped and continue to help.

Thank you to everyone who has been part of my new journey of learning who Christ is in my life: love, grace, and mercy. Along with knowing that I am God's daughter whom He loves.

CONTENTS

FOREWORD

Jean Davis came into my office at the Pregnancy Resource Center. Weary and worn by the effects of her life filled with abuse, abandonment, and self-destructive behaviors. She was so thirsty for the Love of God and accepted Christ into her life even before We finished reading the Scriptures.

Knowing it would mean a commitment and a whole new life path. Her decision to follow Christ altered her future drastically. Not only hers but her son's. It has been an honor to walk with Jean watching God's transforming love radically change her and mold her into the image of Christ,

She is inspirational when she shares what Christ has done in her life. Her heart is to share Christ and assist other women in breaking free from the bondage of sex trafficking, drugs, and self-destructive behavior.

Phyllis Phelps
Executive Director
House of Hope NH, Swanzey, New Hampshire

EDITOR'S NOTE

I first met Jean through our mutual friend, Phyllis Phelps, whose book and audiobook, *Weathering the Storm*, I helped edit and produce.

When I first read Jean's original book, *No More Games*, I was shocked by all she had been through and escaped through God's mercy and grace. Her heart's desire was to use her story to help others escape being trafficked while interweaving the stories of the women in the Bible with her own. In the following pages, you'll see how God intervened in Jean's life. He protected her from death and brought the right people into her life to introduce her to the Savior, Jesus Christ.

It has been my privilege to help Jean tell her story and those of the amazing women in the Bible. They all found encouragement, hope, strength for the journey, and salvation in *El Roi* (The God Who Sees Me) and *Jehovah Rapha* (The LORD our Healer).

As you read this book, I pray you find strength and hope in your journey, despite whatever circumstances you may find yourself in. Most of all, I hope you will trust the Savior, Jesus Christ, and turn to Him.

Dave Ficere
Phoenix, Arizona
January 30, 2023

INTRODUCTION

In this book, you'll get a glimpse of my life in the world of sex trafficking, one of the four major components of human trafficking both in the United States and worldwide. Sex, child, organ, and labor trading all fall under the umbrella of human trafficking. Every woman, man, and child set free from this world has a different story and a unique experience. Many people have entered it after being kidnapped. Still, there are many other ways people come into the life I call "The Game." Some were brought up in this life, and others were coerced and misled into thinking it was something it was not. Sadly, I met women over 40 and as young as 14 when I was in "The Game."

Understand that I am an American citizen, born and raised in the United States. Unfortunately, many people believe those they meet who have come out of human trafficking are from a different country. However, that is not always the case. In 2020, just over 51,000 people reached out to the National Human Trafficking Hotline in one way or another. But there are more people who are silent than who are not, especially those who have had a relationship involving domestic violence. As a result, there are more than three million women involved in human trafficking in the United States and over one million children that have fallen victim to this sick twisted life.

The U.S. Department of Justice defines it this way:

> *"Human trafficking, also known as trafficking in persons, is a crime that involves compelling or coercing a person to provide labor or services or to engage in commercial sex acts. The coercion can be subtle or overt, physical or psychological. Exploitation of a minor for commercial sex is human trafficking, regardless of whether any form of force, fraud, or coercion was used."*

While that is all true, if you ask someone who has been able to be set free from that life, they will tell you it is our modern-day slavery. This beast that has taken over this nation does not care if you are rich or poor, Black, White, Latino, Asian, a boy, girl, man, or woman. It does not care if you come from a two-parent or single-parent home or if you have family members who are alive or not. All it cares about is how much money a person can make for those in charge. You become a product to be purchased by the highest bidder.

You will hear people refer to themselves as survivors of human trafficking. However, as you read my story, you will notice I say I am not a survivor because it took me almost twenty years to get out. Instead, I refer to myself as an overcomer. That is because Jesus Christ saved me and set me free so I could share my story. I also hope to shed some light on a dark world that many people don't understand because Hollywood glamorizes it through movies like *Pretty Woman*.

After reading this book, I pray that you will help save someone's daughter, son, mother, brother, sister, cousin, aunt, uncle, or grandmother from a life of bondage. I pray this book will move you to open your eyes to see what is going on around you to the point that you will want to make a difference in your community, state, and nation.

We need to save women, men, and children from this modern-day slavery in a country that claims to be free.

CHAPTER 1

LOOKING FOR LOVE

Have you ever wanted something in your life so desperately that you would do anything to obtain it? As far as I can remember, there have only been two things in this world I have ever wanted. Like everyone, the first thing is love. The second is acceptance from someone who would tell me I'm part of their family, circle of friends, or you name it.

Growing up, I was not like all the other girls in school with a coke bottle shape. I was short and overweight. I longed to be loved by a man but couldn't find it. In high school, so many girls are insecure about themselves, comparing how they look with others so they can be seen by a boy in school. When I think of ancient times, there was a woman that felt the same way I did. Her name was Leah.

Genesis 29:16-17 tells her story:

> *"And Laban had two daughters: the name of the elder was Leah, and the name of the younger was Rachel. Leah was tender eyed; but Rachel was beautiful and well favoured." (KJV)*

Jacob did not want Leah. He loved Rachel, but Jacob was deceived by Laban and given Leah instead of Rachel after working for seven years. It wasn't until Jacob's wedding night he discovered that Rachel was not the woman he married. Consequently, Jacob was mad at Laban because he did not love Leah. Like any teenage girl, Leah desired to be loved by someone and would do anything to receive that attention. When you read more about Leah's life, you learn more about her thinking.

Now he will love me because I have given him a son, Leah thought every time she had a child by Jacob.

I also went looking for love in all the wrong places, entering a world I wished I had never stepped into. My name is Jean Davis. I was eighteen when I officially became a prostitute, lady of the night, hooker—whatever you want to call me. That is what you think I am. In reality, I was a scared girl, alone in a world full of men who beat and raped me. But after having come to know who Jesus Christ is and experiencing his grace toward me, I have learned to forgive myself. "You shall know the truth, and the truth shall make you free" (NKJV) is God's promise in John 8:32.

Looking back at my life, I see how only God saved me from being a prostitute and being groomed as a prostitute for almost two decades in a world known as "The Game." During that time, the Lord Jesus Christ was with me every step of the way, longing for me to come home. "What man of you, having a hundred sheep, if he loses one of them, does not leave the ninety-nine in the wilderness, and go after the one which is lost until he finds it?" (NKJV) Jesus asks in Luke 15:4. I was that lost sheep.

One day, after I had just gotten out of work, some friends told me about a party they said I needed to attend. I struggled to decide whether to go when my friends finally persuaded me. When I walked in the door, there were women playing chess, drinking, popping ecstasy pills, and smoking weed. In the back room, you could hear people having sex.

"What kind of party is this?" I asked.

"It's a sex party," one guy answered.

That was my introduction to the world of prostitution, which has been around since the dawn of time. Looking back, I think of Rahab and how she grew up in a culture where nothing ever changed. Their country was doing the same thing repeatedly. That was my life growing up. Nothing ever changed. In all honesty, it got worse before it got better. By the time I became an adult of legal age, the culture in my life was just like Rahab's, which was doing the same thing repeatedly. To the point that I didn't know who Jean Davis was. The abuse made me numb and hard to it all, whether physical, mental, emotional, or spiritual.

The Hebrew word used to describe Rahab in Joshua 2:1 literally means "a prostitute woman." However, in some rabbinic texts, she is described as an "innkeeper." Josephus mentions that Rahab kept an inn but is silent about whether merely renting out rooms was her only source of income. It was common for an inn and a brothel to operate within the same building. In the New Testament, the Epistle of James and the Epistle to the Hebrews follow the tradition set by the translators of the Septuagint in using the Greek word usually translated as "harlot" or "prostitute to describe Rahab.

When all you know is being displayed on TV, in magazines, in the streets, and in your family, you will do anything to be accepted by your peers, family, and so-called friends. Until one day when your whole life comes down around you. Your family has written you off as dead. Your friends want nothing to do with you because you have nothing to give them. The streets look at you as damaged goods, and you have no energy to live.

I also went looking for love in all the wrong places.

Sometime later, I decided I was done living like this. I called my parents, crying and begging them to let me come home. My father asked me where I was and told me to sit there and not move. An hour went by, and no sign of my pimps. Finally, my family showed up with some people carrying serious heat to ensure that nothing would happen if anyone came while I was packing my stuff. My father kept telling me to hurry up so we didn't have to deal with the pimps if they returned.

After my family brought me home, I went into my room and put my stuff down.

"Can I take a shower,"? I asked my mother.

"Of course," she replied. "You don't have to ask.

After I was done and dressed, my family asked me if I could come out to the family room so we could talk.

"So, what happened?" my father asked.

The tear started flowing as I began telling how I got involved with having sex for money.

"I don't want to have this discussion today," my mother interrupted, and I stopped talking. Another week went by before anyone spoke about being a "streetwalker," as my mother called me. Then one night, my mother sat down on the couch.

"Do you remember leaving a message on my phone?" she asked.

"It sounded like you didn't know you were leaving a message, and we heard your entire conversation," my dad chimed in.

I started crying as I remembered the night they were talking about. I was trying to get a truck driver to pay me $400 for my services, and an argument ensued. *How could I ever look my parents in the eyes again*? I wondered.

All I wanted was the chance to have hope, just like Rahab. She knew there was hope and something different out there than the life she had been living.

The Bible records her story in Joshua 2:1-13:

> *"Now Joshua the son of Nun sent out two men from Acacia Grove to spy secretly, saying, 'Go, view the land, especially Jericho.' So they went and came to the house of a harlot named Rahab and lodged there. And it was told the king of Jericho, saying, 'Behold, men have come here tonight from the*

children of Israel to search out the country.' So the king of Jericho sent to Rahab, saying, 'Bring out the men who have come to you, who have entered your house, for they have come to search out all the country.' Then the woman took the two men and hid them. So she said, 'Yes, the men came to me, but I did not know where they were from. And it happened as the gate was being shut, when it was dark, that the men went out. Where the men went, I do not know; pursue them quickly, for you may overtake them.' (But she had brought them up to the roof and hidden them with the stalks of flax, which she had laid in order on the roof.) Then the men pursued them by the road to the Jordan, to the fords. And as soon as those who pursued them had gone out, they shut the gate. Now before they lay down, she came up to them on the roof, and said to the men: 'I know that the Lord has given you the land, that the terror of you has fallen on us, and that all the inhabitants of the land are fainthearted because of you. For we have heard how the Lord dried up the water of the Red Sea for you when you came out of Egypt, and what you did to the two kings of the Amorites who were on the other side of the Jordan, Sihon and Og, whom you utterly destroyed. And as soon as we heard these things, our hearts melted; neither did there remain any more courage in anyone because of you, for the Lord your God, He is God in heaven above and on earth

> *beneath. Now therefore, I beg you, swear to me by the Lord, since I have shown you kindness, that you also will show kindness to my father's house, and give me a true token, and spare my father, my mother, my brothers, my sisters, and all that they have, and deliver our lives from death.'"* (NKJV)

Rahab wanted the chance to be set free from the bondage of darkness. The opportunity to truly experience a life of freedom and know what true love looks like. And, like Rahab, I longed to experience grace, mercy, and freedom. I knew that everything I had done in life, the decisions I had made, and what had happened to me by people I trusted or crossed my path did not qualify me to have anything but pain and suffering. Yet, all that experience leads to that one moment in time that changes your whole life story.

CHAPTER 2

BACK TO SCHOOL

I had only been at my parent's house for two days before I started getting death threats from the men I left. One said he knew my parents and would kill them if I did not return to him. Several others told me they would kill me if they saw me on the street. So, for six months, I hid in my parent's house, but as time passed, I was able to leave, go to church with them, and start looking for a job. I pretended that what I had experienced was a dream or like something in the movies. Finally, I was able to get two jobs, one at a gas station and the other at a Waffle House. While everything was going well in the beginning, while staying with my parents, I still felt as if something was missing.

In addition, things at home were starting to get back to the "normal" of my father yelling at me.

"Do something with your life," he would say. My mother was no better.

"What made you think these men would care about you? Look at you. You are fat. What makes you think a man would want to be with a girl that is loose and sloppy?"

The name-calling and belittling of what I looked like came in full force as the physical and mental abuse intensified. Finally, it got to the point where I started asking myself, *How do I get out of this?*

One sunny afternoon while my father was in his office working, he called me in to talk about my future. I had never thought about what I would do next after returning home.

"You can't continue living in our house if you don't have a plan," he said. "Maybe you should start going to college." He also made it clear he was not happy that I listened to my mother and took a year off after graduating high school.

Once again, being a lost puppy looking for love and approval, I reluctantly agreed to attend a junior college to please my father. Unfortunately, I hated school, and anything having to do with learning was not my cup of tea. My father and other family members had always told me that I was not smart enough and that the only thing I would ever be good at in life was lying on my back.

"It's either college or be put back out on the streets," my father added.

> *This is my last chance for my parents to help me before I completely burn that bridge, I thought. So, as any wise person would do, I chose college.*

After a difficult process, including the beatings from my father as a "motivation" to ensure I passed the placement test, I tried my hardest to pick the "right" classes because I did not want to make him mad.

"You need to make enough money to take care of us when we are older, or you will have amounted to nothing," he constantly told me.

Consequently, the classes I wanted to take had to be approved by my father, so I enrolled at Georgia Perimeter College, a part of Georgia State University. My parents also laid out strict rules about using their car. I was to go to school and then straight home, and since I wasn't working, that sounded fine.

I did great the first semester, following their rules and only focusing on my classes and homework. I got a couple of C's and a few B's, which I thought were pretty good for my first time in college. I did not pay any attention to the men roaming the campus and was being the obedient daughter, my father said I needed to be.

"The more obedient you are, the greater chances you can find a husband," he had once told me. That tape constantly echoed in my mind.

One great thing about going to school was meeting some people that seemed cool to hang out with. But I learned when the spring semester started that things were different from high school. I thought college was like high school and assumed I would see the same people from last semester. I did not realize that new people enroll every semester, and some leave. Guys I had never seen before were now on campus, many looking like Denzel Washington or Morris Chestnut. I had to convince myself not to look at them or say anything, so I could remain focused on my classes.

> I couldn't get my heart to stop racing.

A few weeks into the spring semester, I decided I needed to earn some money because I was tired of asking my parents for handouts. They happily reminded me about borrowing from them and even kept track of how much I owed them. When I approached my parents about getting a part-time job, they said I could get a job at the Four Seasons hotel in Atlanta. There was one condition: I would start paying them back $50 per paycheck. I agreed to their condition, went to the hotel, and applied for a job. It just so happened that the hotel staff was doing onsite interviews, and I was offered a job on the spot as the mid-shift receptionist. It worked perfectly with my school schedule.

After working at the hotel for about four months, I had a set routine. During my breaks, I would always go out to my car to do some homework, read my textbooks, go over my lecture notes, and have a cigarette. Everyone knew my routine, but this shift had a lot of interruptions, making it difficult for me to take my break on time. So, I opted not to take my break that night.

The next evening was brisk as I stepped outside for my break from work, not knowing that this night would change everything in my life forever. I was walking to my car to have a cigarette and study for the midterm I was having on Friday.

Looking down at my phone as I walked, I suddenly collided with a man, unsure if I walked into him or he into me.

In any case, he knocked me over so hard that I almost fell to the ground. As he reached out to catch me, I looked up into his eyes, and all of my insides melted. He lifted me up, asking, "Are you okay?"

I was speechless.

"Are you okay?" he repeated.

"Yes, I'm fine," I finally replied.

"Next time, we both need to watch where we're walking so we won't bump into each other again," he laughed.

> *I couldn't get my heart to stop racing when this mystery man went into the hotel. After I was through with my break, I went back inside, hoping to see him again. I couldn't stop thinking about this mystery man. What was his name? Where did he come from? Was he in a relationship, or was he single? Would I ever see him again? All these questions swirled through my head. My focus began shifting from school to finding out who this guy was. A week went by, and I still could not get this mystery man out of my mind! I would do anything to see him again.*

Shortly after, I was getting ready to get off work one rainy, cold night as the night shift was coming in when out of nowhere, the mystery man walked in! My whole body quickly started to melt. I stood there, memorized how he looked and began to check him out. He was about six feet tall and almost looked like a football linebacker. He had hazel eyes with a tint of blue to them and smooth caramel-colored skin. He had a taper fade cut, along with a trimmed goatee. He looked at my name tag while walking up to the front desk.

"Hello Jean, you look beautiful tonight," he said. I smiled and shook my head.

"Have I said something wrong?" he asked.

I was at a loss for words for a couple of seconds. Finally, I exhaled and mustered up the courage to speak.

"Hello, my name is Jean. You look handsome as well, Mister…"

"Kenny Jackson, but people that know me call me Kenny."

"Well, it's nice to meet you, Kenny."

At that moment, Kenny and I locked eyes, and he asked if I would like to join him for the rest of the night so we could get to know each other. I thanked him for the invitation and told him I needed to be somewhere. I didn't want to tell him I had a curfew and needed to run home. Something about this man made me want to look like I was an independent woman. Kenny was disappointed and reluctantly accepted my answer and instead gave me his phone number.

I had not been in a relationship for over a year. I felt like I was going crazy and lacking any adventure living a "square" life with my parents. That night, when I was home in my room, I thought about how amazing it would be if I were Kenny's woman. After I finished dreaming of the exciting things that would happen if I were his woman, I became determined to have Kenny as my man.

CHAPTER 3

KENNY

The next night Kenny walked in and approached the front desk. I was on my lunch break when Tiffany came into the break room.

"There's a guy asking for you."

"Who would be asking for me?"

"A fine Black man."

I jumped up immediately and hurriedly put myself together. Tiffany looked at me and shook her head. "Girl, why you trippn' over this negro?" she asked. "A classy woman doesn't show that they are interested. You want this boy to think you are not into him like that. He is going to think you are easy or something. Take your time, and don't rush out there. If he really wants to see you, he'll wait, so give it about four minutes before you come out."

"Okay, only if you think that is going to work," I replied hesitantly. I waited for about three minutes before walking out and saw him standing there, holding flowers.

"Hello, Jean. I was hoping you were going to be working tonight. I wanted to see if you would like to come with me to a party?"

I was so taken aback. What kind of person comes up to someone they have only spoken to once, maybe twice, and ask them out to a party?

"I don't know you well enough to go to a party with you," I replied, "and besides, I can't go because I am still working."

"Okay, since you don't want to go to the party with me, will you go to dinner instead?"

While Kenny was speaking, it was as if I had gone into a daze. All I could see was his lips moving but nothing else. Finally, Tiffany nudged my arm, startling me out of my fog.

"I'm sorry, can you repeat that? I didn't quite get that," I asked.

Kenny then asked again if I would be comfortable going out with him to dinner, asking me what time I was getting off work. Before I could even get in a word, he interrupted me to the point that I couldn't say anything.

"I'll be back later to pick you up."

"Nah, I'm busy after work," I replied.

"What night aren't you busy to go out with me"? he asked, leaning over the desk.

The way his eyes looked at me and the way he moved his lips made my body melt right there. I reminded myself how I was determined to have him as my man, but I did not want to look desperate. On the contrary, I wanted to make him work in trying to have me. But, after two minutes, he licked his lips, smiled, and said, "All I wanted to do was get to know you. That's it."

I fell into his trap and agreed to meet him the next day. I explained he needed to be at my job by five o'clock in the evening or I was not going anywhere with him. He tried to hand me the flowers.

"No, thank you," I told him.

"Take them and do whatever you want with them," he replied.

I knew if I didn't take them, his friends would be laughing at him. A couple of them were standing by the door, waiting. He leaned over, kissed my hand, and told me I needed to "dress nice for him." I smiled and told him I would see what I had to wear.

The minute he left and was out of sight, I was beside myself. I had never had a man speak to me in a way that made me feel so good and special. I told Tiffany he was the one I would do anything for. I would never have said those words if I knew what would happen next.

I would never have said those words if I knew what would happen next.

Have you tried everything you can think of to fit in? To be part of something? To feel accepted because you feel alone and unwanted. This is how I have felt all my life; I believe that is how the woman in the Bible felt. Who is this woman at the well? You can find her in the gospel of John Chapter 4 of the Bible. The entire chapter is dedicated to this woman, whose name we don't even know. We aren't told anything about her family life. All we know is that she was drawing water in the middle of the day, and Jesus met her when no one wanted to be around her. During his encounter with her, we find out that she is not married and has been with five different men. He tells her all about her life and then reveals that He is the Messiah.

After the encounter, you don't hear about her anywhere else in the Bible. So, at first glance, you might think she is not as important as Rahab, Ruth, or even Mary Magdalen. But you must remember that the Bible is "living and powerful, and sharper than any two-edged sword, piercing even to the division of soul and spirit, and of joints and marrow, and is a discerner of the thoughts and intents of the heart." (Hebrews 4:12, NKJV). When we read the Word of God, we are called to apply it in our lives.

What makes this woman at the well so important to have her story in the Bible? She is relatable, and I know I felt like she did when I met Jesus. She was tired, not wanting to be judged, and longing to feel wanted, accepted, and part of a family that cared for and loved her. The first thing you learn about her is that she is a Samaritan. What is a Samaritan? In ancient times Samaritans were half Jews and half gentile (Assyrians). Even though everyone knew they were half Jewish, Samaritans were not accepted by their Jewish community. The Jews thought Samaritans were unclean, and anything they touched was unclean for the Jews to handle.

Take a moment to think about that. Step into this woman's shoes and imagine growing up not fitting in when, like any child, all she longs for is to be part of their family. Imagine feeling rejected and unwanted by your aunts, uncles, cousins, and even grandparents. She realizes her status in life when she asks Jesus, "How is it that You, being a Jew, ask a drink from me, a Samaritan woman?" For Jews have no dealings with Samaritans." (John 4:9, NKJV).

This was my life growing up. I am Latino and African American. Growing up, I was rarely around my African American family, so at a young age, all I knew was my Latino family and culture. But one day, I was called out and told that I was not Latino. I was made fun of because I was too dark to be a Latino but too light to be an African American. I only had one grandparent I grew up with, but they felt guilty because the family didn't want anything to do with me. Just like the woman at the well.

CHAPTER 4

THE DATE

I had to figure out how to make this date with Kenny happen. My work shifts normally lasted until six o'clock, but I knew there was no way I could go out on a date with Kenny and get home by seven o'clock. By this time, I had become good at lying and manipulating situations to work for me, so the only thing I could think of was to lie to my parents.

"Work called and asked if I could cover a shift," explaining that I would be through with work at eleven o'clock.

Since I had all my school homework done, and I was doing okay in my classes, my father said I could cover the shift that night.

"I'll be home around midnight," I said, knowing it was cutting it close trying to get to Atlanta. The five o'clock traffic on a Friday night was starting to get bad, but I was able to make it to my job site with thirty minutes to spare.

Once I reached work, I had enough time to run to the bathroom and change into the dress I had just gotten from Fifth Avenue and my eight-inch stilettos. I saw Kenny at the front desk asking for me the minute I walked out of the bathroom.

"Oh, she's not working today," one of my co-workers teased, "but if you turn around, you'll see her standing right behind you."

He turned around, stunned, and his eyes got big. "You are gorgeous," was all he could say.

When I saw him, my knees buckled, and all I could do was smile. He was dressed to the nines in his Armani suit, a fresh haircut, and looking finer than ever. It was almost like I was looking at a darker version of Vin Diesel or Dwayne Johnson with hair.

"Are you ready to go? I asked, but Kenny just stood there.

"Swirl around for me, and let me take a good at you," he responded. I hesitated for a moment before my girlfriend Tiffany jumped in. "Show him what you workin' with, girl! We ain't ever seen you dressed up before. We all want to see how you look, girl," she chimed in.

I just put my head down and shook it. I wasn't trying to be a model for anyone, but because Tiffany and Kenny had put me on the spot, I did what they asked me to do. When I was done, Kenny grabbed my waist, pulled me in, and kissed me. My knees locked to the point that I almost fell over, but he held me tighter to ensure I didn't fall.

"Are you okay?" he asked because it seemed that whenever he came around, I was always falling or running into him. At that moment, I didn't know how to handle what had just happened to me. Should I slap him for kissing me or kiss him back? Instead, I held it together, to everyone's surprise.

"You must be someone important because if anyone else tried to pull that kind of stunt, they would have been slapped, yelled at, and got thrown out of the building," Tiffany told Kenny.

I politely and calmly said to Kenny, "Please don't ever kiss me again unless you ask me for a kiss. I am not trying to move fast in this thing we have going on, whatever it may be. I'm not a hood rat or female that will take anything from a man." Immediately, Kenny's attitude changed a bit. He then grabbed my hand, and we walked out of the hotel.

A car was waiting for us, but I got a bad vibe. "I'm not comfortable getting into a car with you. Why don't we walk instead?" I told him. "Or we can take my car," I added, wanting to feel like I was in control of the date, throwing him a look of disdain like he was the biggest fool in the world. I wanted to hold all the cards, so if I was not digging Kenny, I could leave him with the bill and cutout at any point. He looked at me as if he knew what I was doing and agreed to let me drive my car.

As we started to walk away from his car, he turned around and told the men he was with him to follow us to the restaurant. When we arrived and sat down for dinner, I told him, "I have to leave by eleven o'clock."

He started to ask why. I added that I needed to get home by midnight.

Kenny started to laugh. "Are you serious? Do you have a curfew or kids that you have to get home for?"

"What do I look like? I'm only nineteen years old, so no, I don't have any children, and I am not planning on having any anytime soon," I snapped, annoyed at the conversation.

He leaned in over the table and asked again., "Why do you have a time limit on this date?"

"Wouldn't you like to know?" I said playfully.

"Are you trying to play me or something?" he responded, leaning back in his chair.

"How old are you?" I asked, quickly turning the conversation around. I learned that he was 26 years old, had two kids, and worked at Piedmont hospital as a nurse. The man driving the other car was his cousin, and the car was Kenny's. The more we talked at dinner, the more I was falling for him. Everything I was looking for in a man was sitting right in front of me, or so I thought.

Everything I was looking for in a man was sitting right in front of me, or so I thought.

Ever since I was a young teenager, I had a list of things I had to have in the kind of man I wanted to be with. So, talking to him was almost like an interview. I was making Kenny give me his resume to see if he qualified. It was as if he knew exactly what I wanted to hear and how I wanted to hear it.

He reached over the table, grabbed my hand, pulled it up to his mouth, and spoke.

"You are the most beautiful woman I have ever seen," he said. Then he kissed my hand and held on to it for a little longer, and I didn't want him to let go. He could see it on my face.

It was a little past eight p.m. when Kenny asked the waiter for the bill. Which, mind you, was shocking to me because no man had ever paid for anything for me. "Are you ready to go?" he asked.

"Sure. Where are we going now?" I replied.

"Shh, I need you not to ask any more questions for the rest of the night," Kenny responded.

A warning bell went off within my spirit, but I ignored it. I wanted him in the worst way. I wanted to be his girlfriend, even to the point, if I played my cards right, his wife-to-be. So, I went along with it. Kenny explained he would tell me how to get to the destination where we needed to be and that I just needed to be quiet when we got there.

Before I knew it, two guys got in the back seat of my car, and Kenny hopped into the front.

"Hey, what are you…?" I started to ask Kenny about the men when he interrupted me.

"Remember, be quiet."

Thirty minutes later, we pulled up to a mansion where I was next to several luxury cars. A Lamborghini, Jaguar, Aston, Bugatti, Bentley, and my dream car, a Maserati.

"Get out," Kenny said as I turned off the car's engine and stepped out. "You're certainly dressed for the occasion," he added, walking around to the driver's side.

I had no idea what he meant by that until I walked through the front door. There, I saw several women in various stages of dress, and I started crying. At that moment, I knew I was at a high-scale party, most likely sponsored by an escort service. An escort service is a business that provides women for male clients, usually for sexual favors. The agency typically arranges a meeting between one of its women and the client at the customer's house or hotel room (out-call) or the escort's residence (in-call). Some agencies also provide companions for longer durations who may stay with the client or travel on a holiday or business trip. While the escort agency is paid a fee for this booking and dispatch service, the customer must negotiate any additional fees or arrangements directly with the woman for anything else not provided by the agency, usually involving sexual services.

All I could do was stand there and act like I was going to enjoy being there. But all the while, I was thinking, *Why do I get myself involved with these kinds of men?* Finally, I turned around to walk out the door, but Kenny aggressively grabbed me.

"You're trying to leave before I said it was, okay?" he said in a mean tone. "I will beat you and see to it that you are held by some of the men in this room," he snarled. I knew I had to come up with a story to escape the house.

"I can stay, but I need to leave by ten o'clock," I said. Kenny looked at me like I was crazy and shook his head "no."

"Fine," I said, "then know that my parents will call the police if I am not home when I told them I was going to be."

"You're lying," he snapped back.

"No, my parents will report the car I am driving as stolen."

"That isn't your car?" he asked, his eyes getting big, "Girl, did you set me up? Who do you think you are?"

"No, I didn't set you up. I was covering my back. Just in case something like this happened to where I didn't want to be with you anymore, I didn't have to feel invisible."

"You can leave, but before you go, I'm going to show you off."

"What do you mean show me off? I'm not your trophy or your souvenir," as I rolled my eyes at him.

He raised his hand to me and said, "Do it, or your eyes are going to be in the back of your head!"

Why is it every fine-looking man I meet always ends up being some kinda pimp? I asked myself. I felt like a piece of meat once again. Before I walked into the room, I closed my eyes and whispered, "God save me." I exhaled and began walking into the family room, full of raucous men howling, taunting, and jeering at the women who walked across the floor as if it was a runway.

Finally, after I had been shown off to everyone and every disgusting hand had touched me, Kenny allowed me to go. I walked as quickly as I could to my car. I wanted to leave and pretend I had never met Kenny before. But, suddenly, right before I could pull out of the driveway, he was standing in front of my car and walking toward the driver's window.

"I'll be seeing you soon," he said.

"Don't bother. I'm not interested in seeing you after what you just had me do." I rolled up my window and sped out of the driveway, leaving the smell of burning rubber behind.

As I was driving home, all I could think about was why I allowed myself to be put in that position again. I drove in silence, not even turning on the radio, thinking, hoping, and praying that I would never see Kenny again.

CHAPTER 5

JUST LIKE HAGAR

Looking back on my relationship with Kenny, I think of Hagar. She was an Egyptian slave to Abraham and Sarah, most likely given to Abraham when he left Egypt. What is a slave? It is someone who works very hard for long hours or under difficult conditions or is held in forced servitude and completely subservient to a dominating influence.

So, when Sarah (Sarai) told Hagar to sleep with her husband Abraham (Abram), as recorded in Genesis 16, it wasn't as if Hagar had a choice. As a slave, Hagar had to do what she was told. The idea of Hagar becoming a concubine and surrogate mother was probably appealing to her as it certainly would have raised her status.

When I first met Kenny, I thought I would be someone important in his life. To the point where I was willing to make him money, unaware that in every relationship between a pimp and a hoe, there is always what we call "the honeymoon phase." However, there comes a point when the honeymoon ends, and reality settles in. In "The Game," it was all about performance. If the other girls or I didn't meet our quota, didn't perform well, or took too long to get the money, the pimp would get rid of us. By that, I mean suffering the consequence of not following the instructions given by your "daddy." What I mean are a few things that could result in you being beaten, sold to another person, abandoned, or left for dead. All of which happened to me.

I entered "The Game," becoming a slave to a world that would be any normal person's nightmare or something out of a Hollywood movie. After a while, you do things you become ashamed of and feel guilty about. Hagar was prideful at the beginning of her pregnancy, thinking she was important in Abraham's life because of the child she was carrying. She mocked Sarah.

That is until Sarah tired of Hagar and got rid of her.

We read their story in Genesis 16:5-14:

> *"Then Sarai said to Abram, 'My wrong be upon you! I gave my maid into your embrace; and when she saw that she had conceived, I became despised in her eyes. The Lord judge between you and me.' So Abram said to Sarai, 'Indeed your maid is in your hand; do to her as you please.' And when Sarai dealt harshly with her, she fled from her*

presence. Now the Angel of the Lord found her by a spring of water in the wilderness, by the spring on the way to Shur. And He said, 'Hagar, Sarai's maid, where have you come from, and where are you going?' She said, 'I am fleeing from the presence of my mistress Sarai.' The Angel of the Lord said to her, 'Return to your mistress, and submit yourself under her hand.' Then the Angel of the Lord said to her, 'I will multiply your descendants exceedingly, so that they shall not be counted for multitude.' And the Angel of the Lord said to her: 'Behold, you are with child, And you shall bear a son. You shall call his name Ishmael because the Lord has heard your affliction. He shall be a wild man; His hand shall be against every man, And every man's hand against him. And he shall dwell in the presence of all his brethren.' Then she called the name of the Lord who spoke to her, You-Are-the-God-Who-Sees; for she said, 'Have I also here seen Him who sees me?' Therefore the well was called Beerlahairoi; observe, it is between Kadesh and Bered." (NKJV)

And, just like Hagar crying out to God and seeing that Yahweh truly saw her, there comes a point in your life when you feel that the only thing you can do is cry out and ask, "God, do you see me? I'm done with living this kind of life. I can't continue living like this." It's the breaking point where you feel so weak and vulnerable that you want things to change. That is where Hagar was when Yahweh saw her, reassured her, and told her that her son would also become a nation.

> I entered "The Game," becoming a slave to a world that would be any normal person's nightmare.

A woman walks up and down a street to get a date because they have their trafficker (pimp) watching to see if they will make their quota for the night. Meanwhile, you have other women, and people generally look at you as if you are a disease or something that will kill them with a disease. Yes, some people involved in human trafficking become HIV or Hep C positive. But why do others treat people like they have a plague? Perhaps they don't understand that some people like me had no choice but to do what we were told because a pimp with a gun was watching and threatening your life if you did not come back with some money.

When I tell people I am an overcomer of human trafficking, their reaction hurts me the most. Some take a step backward and say things like, "really?" or, "I'm sorry, what country are you from?" But the worst reaction is watching their face become scared as if they will catch something in the air by speaking to me. When I tell them that both of my sons are products of human trafficking, they look at them as if they are slime. I hate using the word "survivor" to describe myself because I am not one. Instead, I'm an overcomer because of Jesus Christ. He is who I turned to when I had nowhere to go.

I forgive rather than blame the men that hurt my family or me. When you accept Jesus Christ in your life by not just saying a prayer with someone but embracing Jesus, you learn that Jesus forgave you when He died on the cross, even when you were His foe. He still loved you and me enough to pursue us when no one else wanted us. So, if Jesus can forgive me of all my sins, who am I not to forgive the people that hurt me? As Jesus and later Stephen said, "Forgive them, father, for they do not know what they do."

There are so many people in this world and more here in the United States who do not understand genuinely forgiving people. So many don't understand how women end up in human trafficking because they don't know how to be clean and feel dirty and angry because they have been hurt or abused. We can help these hurting people by getting to the root problem and showing them Jesus. Jesus said that "We are to be in this world but not of this world." We are called to expose the darkness for what it is and share the "good news," the gospel of how Jesus came on this earth to die for our sins and bring us back into a relationship with the Heavenly Father.

My passion is to reach those forgotten and lost in human trafficking and bring them to the grace and freedom only found in a relationship with Jesus Christ as Lord and Savior.

CHAPTER 6

KENNY'S RETURN

Several weeks had gone by since I last heard from Kenny. I thought he had forgotten about me and that I would not have to worry about seeing him again. However, one day I walked out of class to ask a male classmate a question about the lecture. Out of nowhere, Kenny ran up to my friend and started beating him, yelling, "stay away from my girl."

"Stop, get off him. He's just a classmate, I screamed at Kenny. "You're crazy," I added as some men from campus security arrived to break things up. I was beside myself.

"What is wrong with you? I yelled, "I'm not your girl. Last time I checked, if I remember correctly, I made it very clear that I never wanted to see you again!"

Kenny told me that I was his and that no man he had "not approved of"' could be talking to me. Then he grabbed me and started to pull me toward the parking lot.

"We are not together, and I'm not your property," I argued. "Who do you think you are coming onto my campus and starting fights with guys you see me talking to?" I was furious and continued my verbal assault. "You've crossed your boundary with me, for real this time. I don't owe you a thing. You have wasted my time, and I'm not into you like that anymore. Your whole attitude of 'it's my way or the beat down way' is so not attractive to me."

I started resisting and pulling away from him, but the look in his eyes told me that would mean trouble. My fear was obvious as he grabbed me by the waist, pulled me in close, and said, "Come on. I have a surprise for you."

I just looked at him. I wanted to say no and tell him to leave me alone, but something inside me was afraid to speak up. A part of me felt special when he pulled me close to him, so I kept my mouth shut. Still, all kinds of questions were flying through my mind. *What could he possibly surprise me with? How did he know what school I went to?* I never told him when I attended school or that I would be there on campus.

We walked across campus toward the parking lot before I got the guts to try and escape. "I have another class that I need to be at today," I told him.

"You're going to skip class. You're coming with me," he sternly replied. The way he was holding on to me made it clear that if I kept arguing with him, I would end up getting a fist to the face. I had been down that road before.

"Where are we going?" I snapped. His response surprised me.

"You are right! We are not together. You're my wifey," he replied matter-of-factly, using the term pimps often use to describe women under their control. My whole heart sunk to the bottom of my stomach, And I felt like throwing up.

Kenny finally let go of me. I ran to the bathroom to wash my face, fully aware he was waiting threateningly outside. As I stared into the mirror, I started to cry. *Am I in a horror movie? What did I get myself into again? Why do I pick these kinds of men? It never fails. It's like I have a big green neon sign across my forehead saying I want men to beat me and make me have sex with hundreds of men that I don't know.*

I was in the bathroom for a while when Kenny walked inside. He asked me what was taking so long. I told him I would be out in a minute, but he would only leave once I left with him. So, I splashed some water on my face again and left the bathroom.

We walked to his car, and he told me to get in. Surprisingly, no one else was in the car. We put on our seat belts, and he leaned over to kiss me on the lips. That was a first because most pimps don't kiss their girls, let alone on the lips. Of the many different pimps I already was involved with, not once would kiss me even if I asked.

When he kissed me, my whole body just melted! There was a cold chill that ran down my spine. I was overwhelmed with childlike laughter and had a smile that I could not get off my face. I asked him where we were going.

"Sit back and shut up," he replied, looking at me.

I was scared, but Kenny held my hand as if I was his woman and the most important person in his world. So, I kept my composure until we pulled up to a house. As he parked the car, I looked out the window. I saw a few men standing outside, smoking and drinking.

"Where are we at?" I asked disgustedly.

Kenny raised his hand to me and said, "This is your last warning! What did I tell you? Sit back and shut up! What don't you understand about that statement?

After he was done screaming at me, he parked the car. "Wait in the car. Do not get out until I come back, and don't talk to anybody." He got out of the car and walked up the driveway. I watched him until he disappeared out of sight.

I was in the car for a good hour or so before I saw him come from behind the house. He opened my door and said, "Be quiet. You will speak only when you are spoken to."

I followed Kenny up the driveway. As we walked, we passed some men. They were staring at me, and a couple started whispering. Some were loud enough for me to hear.

When he kissed me, my whole body just melted!

"Damn! Who's the owner of that delicious piece of meat? Where did that piece of skin come from? I want that thick, round piece on me! Who is she? That girl is thick as hell. I want some of that."

It would not stop. They got bolder to the point that one man grabbed my butt. I almost turned around when I felt

Kenny jerk my hand. He gave me that look that said, "I will beat you here in front of these men if you make a move." All I could do was put my head down in shame.

It felt like we were never going to make it, but finally, we reached the end of the driveway. A little house was hidden behind what looked like a garage and some bushes. Before we walked in the door, Kenny turned to me and said, "There is no turning back now." Then, he cradled me in his arms and gave me the most passionate, breathtaking kiss. My knees almost gave way, and my legs felt like Jell-O.

When we were done kissing, and while I was still in a daze, he reiterated his demands: "From this point on, unless I say a man can be with you, you are mine and nobody else's." Then, he added, "Whatever happens in this house stays in this house. You do what I say. And you obey whoever I say you have to listen to."

My heart felt as heavy as rocks as it sunk into my stomach. I started to ask him a question. "So, does that...." I began asking, but he didn't even give me time to finish asking the question before reaching to open the door.

My eyes scanned the front room of the little house as we walked in. There were about eight Black men inside. One of the men was getting his haircut, and a few were playing at the pool table. Others were sitting on a couch. I looked up and saw mirrors on the ceiling. The minute I looked back at the men sitting on the couch, they stood up. Kenny looked at me and said, "Get ready."

"Get ready for what?" I whispered. My heart started to race, and I began to sweat. My feet became stuck to the floor. It was as if you would get cold feet when getting married.

That is when the words I was dreading to hear him say came out of his mouth: "I'm your daddy."

I looked at him and said, "How are you going to claim me when you have never had me before?"

In an instant, one of his hands was around my throat, and he started to squeeze. "Don't question me ever! This is how we are about to play this game. Not only am I going to have you, but some of these men are too. You're right. You can't call me daddy until I have you, so you're going to do everything I tell you I want you to do. If you pass this test, we won't beat you."

I had committed a cardinal sin by questioning him in front of the other men. Panic-stricken, I had an idea.

"I must be at work tonight and can't afford to lose my job because my parents would kick me out. Do you have a place for me to live?"

The next thing I remember is holding my cheek and looking at my hand. It had blood on it because Kenny's "boy" Roy had hit me with a pistol after I challenged Kenny by

talking back. I had to be put in my place and be shown that anyone Kenny allowed could do anything to me. That included hitting me or abusing my body. I had to think fast about how to get out of the situation.

"How about this? If I pass your test tonight, you bring me back to school, and tomorrow, I will recruit some girls from my college that can take my place. If I don't come through, you and your boys can do whatever you please to even the score."

For some reason, Kenny agreed to my proposal. That night I was forced to sleep with Kenny and four other men, with everything recorded and shared online for others to see. All the while, I had to hold back my tears because no man could see me vulnerable and crying.

When we were finished, Kenny grabbed my hand and led me out of the little house. While we were walking back to the car, I heard the men talking.

"Good pickin', you got a dime piece," one said. "You got an obedient female that will listen to you when you whip her into shape the way she needs to be. That is a loyal dog you have, boy. You need to keep her," another one chimed in.

Kenny tried to lean over for a kiss in the car, but when he saw I was not willing, he grabbed my neck.

"If you ever resist me again, there will be consequences," he warned as we drove off.

CHAPTER 7

RAHAB

Have you ever wanted to be accepted by a group? Or tried to feel like you were part of the crowd of people, whether it was your family or friends? Every time you did or said something wrong, they looked at you like, "what are you doing?" or "why are you here?" In those moments, you feel alone. All the emotions, such as anger, depression, and rejection, come up. After a while, you might either react in violence or self-harm. To the point that others look at you like there is something wrong with you. They want nothing to do with you unless it benefits them.

That is what was going on with the people that came to Rahab. Everyone in the country knew she was a prostitute and wanted nothing to do with her. That is until the word got around that some Israelite men the king had sent were in the city and wanted information from her. Because of her reputation, it was known that men would go see her for service, and that was the only time she was worthy of speaking with or being around. Not because they cared for her as a friend.

We read about Rahab in Joshua 2:1-22:

> *"And Joshua the son of Nun sent out of Shittim two men to spy secretly, saying, Go view the land, even Jericho. And they went, and came into an harlot's house, named Rahab, and lodged there. And it was told the king of Jericho, saying, Behold, there came men in hither to night of the children of Israel to search out the country. And the king of Jericho sent unto Rahab, saying, Bring forth the men that are come to thee, which are entered into thine house: for they be come to search out all the country. And the woman took the two men, and hid them, and said thus, There came men unto me, but I wist not whence they were: And it came to pass about the time of shutting of the gate, when it was dark, that the men went out: whither the men went I wot not: pursue after them quickly; for ye shall overtake them. But she had brought them up to the roof of the house, and hid them with the stalks of flax, which she had laid in order upon the roof. And the men pursued after them the way to Jordan unto the fords: and as soon as they which pursued after them were gone out, they shut the gate. And before they were laid down, she came*

up unto them upon the roof; And she said unto the men, I know that the Lord hath given you the land, and that your terror is fallen upon us, and that all the inhabitants of the land faint because of you. For we have heard how the Lord dried up the water of the Red sea for you, when ye came out of Egypt; and what ye did unto the two kings of the Amorites, that were on the other side Jordan, Sihon and Og, whom ye utterly destroyed. And as soon as we had heard these things, our hearts did melt, neither did there remain any more courage in any man, because of you: for the Lord your God, he is God in heaven above, and in earth beneath. Now therefore, I pray you, swear unto me by the Lord, since I have shewed you kindness, that ye will also shew kindness unto my father's house, and give me a true token: And that ye will save alive my father, and my mother, and my brethren, and my sisters, and all that they have, and deliver our lives from death. And the men answered her, Our life for yours, if ye utter not this our business. And it shall be, when the Lord hath given us the land, that we will deal kindly and truly with thee. Then she let them down by a cord through the window: for her house was upon the town wall, and she dwelt upon the wall. And she said unto them, Get you to the mountain, lest the pursuers meet you; and hide yourselves there three days, until the pursuers be returned: and afterward may ye go your way. And

> *the men said unto her, We will be blameless of this thine oath which thou hast made us swear. Behold, when we come into the land, thou shalt bind this line of scarlet thread in the window which thou didst let us down by: and thou shalt bring thy father, and thy mother, and thy brethren, and all thy father's household, home unto thee. And it shall be, that whosoever shall go out of the doors of thy house into the street, his blood shall be upon his head, and we will be guiltless: and whosoever shall be with thee in the house, his blood shall be on our head, if any hand be upon him. And if thou utter this our business, then we will be quit of thine oath which thou hast made us to swear. And she said, According unto your words, so be it. And she sent them away, and they departed: and she bound the scarlet line in the window." (KJV)*

Rahab knew that there was something different about these men of Israel. Have you ever known someone different who drew you in like a moth to a flame? She wanted something they had that she didn't. Something in her heart was missing. The way the Israelites spoke or looked at her may have made her feel as if she was safe and accepted. She allowed herself to open her heart to Yahweh as we are asked to do in Revelation 3:20, which says, "Behold, I stand at the door, and knock: if any man hear my voice, and open the door, I will come into him, and will sup with him, and he with me." (KJV)

Have you ever known someone different who drew you in like a moth to a flame?

As she embraced their God in faith and recalled the great deeds he had done for the Israelites, she became useful to Yahweh and bore much fruit.

Rahab became a living example of what the apostle wrote about in John 15:1-10:

> *"I am the true vine, and my Father is the husbandman. Every branch in me that beareth not fruit he taketh away: and every branch that beareth fruit, he purgeth it, that it may bring forth more fruit. Now ye are clean through the word which I have spoken unto you. Abide in me, and I in you. As the branch cannot bear fruit of itself, except it abide in the vine; no more can ye, except ye abide in me. I am the vine, ye are the branches: He that abideth in me, and I in him, the same bringeth forth much fruit: for without me ye can do nothing. If a man abide not in me, he is cast forth as a branch, and is withered; and men gather them, and cast them into the fire, and they are burned. If ye abide in me, and my words abide in you, ye shall ask what ye will, and it shall be done unto you. Herein is my Father glorified, that ye bear much fruit; so shall ye be my disciples. As the Father hath loved me, so have I loved you: continue*

ye in my love. If ye keep my commandments, ye shall abide in my love; even as I have kept my Father's commandments and abide in his love." (KJV)

Jesus is the vine, and when you open your heart to Him, he brings you into a relationship of love and acceptance with him. Rahab was not only accepted by the Israelites but became one of the branches as the great-grandmother of Jesus Christ Himself. Think of that! A person that everyone dismissed and rejected became someone important as an ancestor to Jesus Christ. So, when everyone views you as "less than" or not able to amount to anything because of your past (just like the people in Jericho did with Rahab), remember what Paul said to the Corinthians: "But God hath chosen the foolish things of the world to confound the wise; and God hath chosen the weak things of the world to confound the things which are mighty." (1 Corinthians 1:27, KJV).

However, until you come to the end of yourself and have tried (and done) everything, you will be like me, returning to a life you know you don't want to be in your heart. And that was going through my mind when Kenny came back into my life and when I thought I had had enough.

CHAPTER 8

ENOUGH IS ENOUGH

When Kenny and I returned to school, I saw some girls I knew.

"Hey, Jean, where you been?" they yelled.

"Who are they?" Kenny asked me.

"Some of my classmates," I replied. "Why, do you want to jump in and beat them up for talking to me, too?" I added sarcastically.

Wham! The next thing I knew, my head hit the window as Kenny punched me in the mouth for questioning him.

"Never talk to me like that," he told me as I held my mouth and fought back the tears. "I care about you, girl. But damn, every time I turn around, you have a question or statement that is not necessary. Do you understand, Jean? I want you to be my main piece, but you can't talk to me that way. I have to teach you what your place is and what I expect from you."

I wasn't listening to what he was saying. Instead, my mind was trying to figure out how to get out of the car and as far away from Kenny as I could. But, before I could pull myself together and get out of the car, Kenny reached over. I instinctively flinched.

"I am sorry, babe; I will never do that to you again. I just don't like being disrespected," he said softly. Strangely, he also asked for my phone number to keep track of where I was. I almost wanted to give him a fake number but instead gave him my real digits. He called it immediately, right in front of me, so I was glad I didn't lie to him. There's no telling what he might have done to me had I done so. He also asked me to line up some other girls for him, as I had promised to do. Kenny rolled down the window as I opened the door and stepped out of the car.

"Well, I'll need some time because I have never done that before," I replied.

"Okay, I will give you two days. After that, if there are no results, I will have to punish you."

Over the next twenty-four hours, I hustled some girls to come with me to meet Kenny and his friends. I made sure I texted him to let him know that I had Stacy and Lisa ready for him and his boys. Less than two minutes later, I got a phone call from him.

"Bring them to me," he said, and 30 minutes later, the two girls and I were back at the same house Kenny had brought me to.

As I walked up the driveway with Stacy and Lisa, I told them to follow my lead and do whatever I did. Stacy started to ask a question until I gave her a sharp look that made her rethink asking me anything. I never told them what they were walking into.

When we reached the front of the little house, I knocked on the door. Kenny answered and said, "there's my baby girl." He turned around, looked at the men in the room, and said, "didn't I tell y'all I had a bottom?" I walked in with the ladies behind me, and everyone was surprised that I returned with some girls who were ready for a good time. Or at least that is what they thought.

We couldn't make it into the room fast enough before several men started kissing and caressing Stacy and Lisa. Meanwhile, Kenny took me to the backroom, told me that I was his, and he was my daddy, and that there would be rules now since I had proven myself to him and his crew.

I thought I was in for the beating of my life.

Suddenly, one of the girls started screaming, "Get off me. Help!" I jumped up and ran into the other room. I pulled the guy off Lisa and punched him twice in the face. Kenny got in between the guy and me, and I started yelling. "Don't you hear her screaming 'Stop?'" Kenny told me that he would beat me until I was black and blue.

"Not before I call the boys (cops) on you for rape. Enough is enough! The girls and I are out of here."

"What kind of broad (female) did you pick up? You got a girl that is willing to call 5-0," one of Kenny's boys asked him.

My stomach tightened into knots as I thought I was in for the beating of my life. Worse than what my father would give me. That night was the beginning and end of a world I did not want to return to. I dropped the girls off and told them I understood if they didn't want to talk to me again.

They assured me we were still friends, and it meant a lot to them that I would fight a man for them and try to protect them. What they didn't realize was that I put my life in danger because of what I did. I was forced back into a lifestyle that I did not want as a piece of property belonging to someone else. There was no getting away with what I did in that house.

The next day Kenny showed up at my job. "You need to take a break," he said.

"It's not time for my break yet."

"If you don't take a break now, you won't have a job anymore, he said, glaring at me. So, I asked my supervisor if I could take an early break. Tiffany was okay with that since she saw the seriousness of the conversation between Kenny and me.

I came around to the front desk where Kenny was standing. He grabbed me, and we walked to the elevators.

"Where are we going," I asked.

We stepped into the elevator, went up two floors, exited, and walked to a room.

"I didn't know you had a room in the hotel," I said in surprise.

As we walked in, Kenny shoved me, and I was greeted with a fist from his boy, Terrance. After I was punched and had gotten a couple of slaps, Kenny spoke.

"Never confront any of the men in the house or threaten to call the boys on them. The girls you bring to the house better know the rules of the game, or you will be beaten in front of everyone.

At the time, I did not realize that Kenny was getting paid for having me bring the women. Then, one night when I had five girls with me, I saw money being handed to him. Once again, I was surrounded by money but never was allowed to touch any of it.

CHAPTER 9

HANNAH

Would you do anything for love or feel loved? How about wanting to feel important in the eyes of someone who means so much to you? Or wanting to have importance in someone's life but being bullied because you don't have what others have? Unfortunately, all kinds of bullying happen in everyone's life, and it looks different for each person. So, what do you do when this is going on in your life? Well, let's meet a woman that was bullied year after year by someone close to her.

The woman's name was Hannah, one of two women married to a man named Elkanah. It isn't clear in the Scriptures which wife he married first, but Hannah had no children, while his other wife, Peninnah, had many. Having children was an important part of the culture in biblical times, and women were shamed if they could not have a baby. Yet, Hannah's infertility didn't matter to Elkanah. The Bible makes it clear how deeply he loved her and understood the pain she endured from the other wife. Hannah was not only shamed, but Peninnah bullied her for not having a baby.

We read the story in 1 Samuel 1:1-20:

> *"Now there was a certain man of Ramathaim Zophim, of the mountains of Ephraim, and his name was Elkanah the son of Jeroham, the son of Elihu, the son of Tohu, the son of Zuph, an Ephraimite. And he had two wives: the name of one was Hannah, and the name of the other Peninnah. Peninnah had children, but Hannah had no children. This man went up from his city yearly to worship and sacrifice to the Lord of hosts in Shiloh. Also the two sons of Eli, Hophni and Phinehas, the priests of the Lord, were there. And whenever the time came for Elkanah to make an offering, he would give portions to Peninnah his wife and to all her sons and daughters. But to Hannah he would give a double portion, for he loved Hannah, although the Lord had closed her womb. And her rival also provoked her severely, to make her miserable, because the Lord had closed her womb. So it was, year by year, when she went up to the house of the Lord, that she provoked her; therefore she wept and did not eat. Then Elkanah her husband said to her, 'Hannah, why do you*

weep? Why do you not eat? And why is your heart grieved? Am I not better to you than ten sons?' So Hannah arose after they had finished eating and drinking in Shiloh. Now Eli the priest was sitting on the seat by the doorpost of the tabernacle of the Lord. And she was in bitterness of soul, and prayed to the Lord and wept in anguish. Then she made a vow and said, 'O Lord of hosts, if You will indeed look on the affliction of Your maidservant and remember me, and not forget Your maidservant, but will give Your maidservant a male child, then I will give him to the Lord all the days of his life, and no razor shall come upon his head.' And it happened, as she continued praying before the Lord, that Eli watched her mouth. Now Hannah spoke in her heart; only her lips moved, but her voice was not heard. Therefore Eli thought she was drunk. So Eli said to her, 'How long will you be drunk? Put your wine away from you!' But Hannah answered and said, 'No, my lord, I am a woman of sorrowful spirit. I have drunk neither wine nor intoxicating drink, but have poured out my soul before the Lord. Do not consider your maidservant a wicked woman, for out of the abundance of my complaint and grief I have spoken until now.' Then Eli answered and said, 'Go in peace, and the God of Israel grant your petition which you have asked of Him.' And she said, 'Let your maidservant find favor in your sight.' So the woman went her way

> *and ate, and her face was no longer sad. Then they rose early in the morning and worshiped before the Lord, and returned and came to their house at Ramah. And Elkanah knew Hannah his wife, and the Lord remembered her. So it came to pass in the process of time that Hannah conceived and bore a son, and called his name Samuel, saying, 'Because I have asked for him from the Lord.'" (NKJV)*

What do you want so badly that people make fun of you? How about the people who throw the very thing they possess in your face? When I was living in "The Game," I would learn Kenny and the pimps in my life would be married or with someone while I was the girl that just made them money while living in hotel rooms. I knew that every day I was on the verge of being homeless if I didn't go out and make money, not just so I could have a roof over my head but also to ensure I was not going to get beaten for not making money for my pimps. The bullying and taunting miraculously don't go away even after coming out of that lifestyle and becoming a Christian. People throw the very thing you may be praying for back in your face. For example, I have been taunted because I am not married yet. I have been told that no one wants to be with me or even that I am too old to be someone's wife. You name it. In times like these, I think of Hannah and how she went to the temple and prayed to God.

I knew that every day I was on the verge of being homeless if I didn't go out and make money.

If there is anyone that understands what you are going through is a man named Jesus Christ. He was bullied by the people, according to Matthew 27:

> *"Then the soldiers of the governor took Jesus into the Praetorium and gathered the whole garrison around Him. And they stripped Him and put a scarlet robe on Him. When they had twisted a crown of thorns, they put it on His head, and a reed in His right hand. And they bowed the knee before Him and mocked Him, saying, 'Hail, King of the Jews!' Then they spat on Him, and took the reed and struck Him on the head. And when they had mocked Him, they took the robe off Him, put His own clothes on Him, and led Him away to be crucified." (Matthew 27:27-31, NKJV)*

Yes, just like anyone, I get discouraged. The difference is when I was in "The Game," I could not talk to anyone about how I felt because I didn't trust anyone around me. So I just dealt with the pain. When you come to Christ, you can call on Jesus, as the scripture says, "In my distress, I called upon the Lord, and cried unto my God: he heard my voice out of his temple, and my cry came before him, even into his ears." (Psalm 18:6, KJV)

We must remember that we are sinners, "brought forth in iniquity, And in sin my mother conceived me." (Psalm 51:5, NKJV) Because we are sinful people living in a fallen world, there will be times in our lives when people say hurtful things. I have come to realize that when people are hurt, their first instinct is to lash out at others. As the saying goes, "hurt people, hurt people." Often, for Christians, the one thing that you must do is fight against words. In my life, horrific things were done to me physically and emotionally. Still, when you are mentally abused, it takes time to overcome the lies people have spoken about you. In this case, the taunting comes from the people closest to you. People don't like it when you are different or are doing well in their eyes.

Take, for example, Cain and Abel, the first siblings who were spoken about in Scripture, and Adam and Eve's two children. This is what it says in Genesis 4:1-15:

> *"Now Adam knew Eve his wife, and she conceived and bore Cain, and said, 'I have acquired a man from the Lord.' Then she bore again, this time his brother Abel. Now Abel was a keeper of sheep, but Cain was a tiller of the ground. And in the process of time it came to pass that Cain brought an offering of the fruit of the ground to the Lord. Abel also brought of the firstborn of his flock and of their fat. And the Lord respected Abel and his offering, but He did not respect Cain and his offering. And Cain was very angry, and his countenance fell. So the Lord said to Cain, 'Why are you angry? And why has your countenance fallen? If you do well, will you not be accepted? And if you do not do well, sin lies at the door. And its desire is for you, but you should rule over it.' Now Cain talked with Abel his brother; and it came to pass, when they were in the*

> *field, that Cain rose up against Abel his brother and killed him. Then the Lord said to Cain, 'Where is Abel your brother?" He said, 'I do not know. Am I my brother's keeper?' And He said, 'What have you done? The voice of your brother's blood cries out to Me from the ground. So now you are cursed from the earth, which has opened its mouth to receive your brother's blood from your hand. When you till the ground, it shall no longer yield its strength to you. A fugitive and a vagabond you shall be on the earth.' And Cain said to the Lord, 'My punishment is greater than I can bear! Surely You have driven me out this day from the face of the ground; I shall be hidden from Your face; I shall be a fugitive and a vagabond on the earth, and it will happen that anyone who finds me will kill me.' And the Lord said to him, 'Therefore, whoever kills Cain, vengeance shall be taken on him sevenfold.' And the Lord set a mark on Cain, lest anyone finding him should kill him." (NKJV)*

So, when you start to think that no one understands what you are going through, remember there is nothing new under the sun (Ecclesiastes 1:9). Other people before you maynot have gone through the exact situations you are going through at this very moment, but when you read the Bible, you see people in ancient times faced the same core issues you and I now face. Until your eyes are opened to a man named Jesus Christ who can not only show you but walk with you during those times of pain and hurt, you will never experience the freedom that John speaks about: "And ye shall know the truth, and the truth shall make you free." (John 8:32, KJV)

CHAPTER 10

SURPRISE!

I was walking out the door when Kenny stopped me. I confronted him about the money, and he kicked on his charm, sweet-talking me while rubbing my arms and kissing my forehead.

"Babe, babe, wifey, where are you going?" he asked.

"So, all we are is pieces of meat for sale? You get all the profits and not even tell me?" I responded in disgust.

"You weren't supposed to see the 'surprise' I was going to give you," he cooed.

"Why is it that every time I catch you in something, you always say there is a surprise? I don't want your surprises. I'm good off you. For all I care, you can step."

"Come back inside, and let me make it up to you," he said, playing with my hair. I flashed back to when my father would play with my hair before or after beating me, yelling at me for doing something wrong, or after spending time with me. At that very moment, I wanted to vomit. My face got pale white to the point that I pushed Kenny's hand away and stepped back.

Kenny told me I should feel so special and connected with him and that I was his, and he was mine.

It was as if this man was trying to convince me I was the one for him, and he was the one for me. I wanted to believe that I was truly his wife, not his wifey. He whispered everything he could that a 19-year-old girl who had been rejected, dismissed, and abused wanted to hear from the ones she loved.

I felt like a different person when I left Kenny that night. A confident, bold woman who I had never known before. All because Kenny told me at that moment after we had shared intimacy how beautiful I was and the only woman that understood him.

The next few days passed, and I did not hear from Kenny. I would call his cell phone, and there would be no answer. Finally, when it reached the point that his message box was full and could not take any more voice messages. I texted him, but there was no reply. This continued for three weeks while I was becoming lethargic in school and at work because Kenny was not responding to my calls or text messages.

One day, nearly two months later, I was throwing up in the school bathroom. Questions began swirling around in my head. *How could I be pregnant? I am only nineteen. I can't raise a child.* Then my friend Ashley handed me a pregnancy test.

"Take it," she said, "and I will be there for you whatever the outcome is."

I took the test and waited with my eyes closed. Finally, I asked Ashley to read the results back to me.

The words fell from her mouth, "Jean, you are pregnant."

I started crying. "What happens now? I must tell my parents. Kenny has not spoken to me for almost three months. I'm not ready to be a mother! I have no clue what that looks like."

Just then, I heard very faint music. It sounded like Kenny's car.

"Come with me," I told Ashley, "I may need you."

We quickly walked outside. I stopped dead in my tracks as Kenny walked around to the other side of his car to open the door. Stacy got out of the car. An angry rage consumed me as I ran up to the car and laid Stacy out with two sharp blows to the head. I looked at Kenny and, without thinking twice, started pushing and swinging at him. He grabbed me and spun me around, pinning me against the car.

"Who do you think you are to step to me like that? I could have you touched (meaning he could have someone kill me)," he said.

I did not care about being touched because my adrenaline was running so hard. I head-butted Kenny, looked at him, and yelled at him, "You spit in my face," before getting in my car and heading home. As a result of beating Stacy up, I got expelled from school. I cried profusely while driving home.

How am I going to tell my parents? What is going to happen to me? I wondered. My parents were gone when I got home, so I went straight to my room and cried. My phone was going off, but I did not care. I saw my whole world crumbling right before my eyes. Then, suddenly, the door to my room opened, and I heard my mother's voice.

"Are you okay? What's wrong" she asked.

I lied, telling her I was mad about my grade in one of my classes. She told me it would be okay to not worry about anything. I thought it would be that easy. About two weeks later, I was sitting on the couch one evening watching HGTV. My father was on his computer working, and my mother was cooking in the kitchen. Then, out of nowhere, she walked out of the kitchen.

"You are pregnant?" she asked suddenly as she approached me.

"What are you talking about?" I replied, trying to hide it from her.

My mother slapped my face. "Don't lie! You are pregnant!"

My father stopped what he was doing and looked at me with eyes that said, "If you lie to my wife again, I am going to hurt you." So, I dropped my head to my chest, and in a soft voice, I answered, "yes."

My mother slapped my face.
"Don't lie! You are pregnant!"

It had been a couple of weeks since I had seen Kenny. Even when I went to the barbershop to get my hair braided, some people would ask me if I knew where Kenny was. He was not returning my calls, and I had not returned his because I was still furious with him. So, I decided to find another man. I was walking into Foot Locker at the mall to grab some Air Max for myself when the customer rep approached me. His name was Jaquan Adams. After I had purchased the shoes, he asked me if I was with anyone.

"No, I'm single," I told him. He asked for my number to see if we could have dinner or something.

The next night we had dinner at the Cheesecake Factory, and from then on, we were together almost every day. I was trying hard to forget Kenny and everything I felt for him, and Jaquan came along at the right time.

We were together for about two months before I told Jaquan I was pregnant. I spoke to him in such a way that there would be no doubt in his mind that I was pregnant with his baby. However, when some of my aunts, uncles, and other family members discovered what I was trying to do, they told me that I was "acting like a true hood rat" to trap Jaquan because I did not want to deal with Kenny.

"That is beneath the way the family does things," they said. Still, I said nothing. My parents did not know what everyone else in the family knew. Jaquan was not the father. My parents wanted to believe me when I told them it was Jaquan's baby. I did not speak to or see Kenny for the rest of my pregnancy. Finally, I went into labor, and Jaquan showed up at the hospital and stayed until the baby was born.

After I had my son, Jaquan disappeared. My father tried calling him to see when he was coming back to sign the birth certificate. After three days passed with no answer, my father took over and named my son John Davis. When I found out my son's name, I wanted to put my father through a wall because, during my entire childhood, I felt neither wanted nor accepted by my father.

"Your mother tricked me into having a baby because her biological clock was ticking," he would tell me. "I did not want a baby. I did not want a girl, especially you, Jean." I felt if I were going to have a baby, then I would be okay to have a son. And, because I didn't get what I wanted through your mother, I let her pick your name. However, since you were out of it from having the baby and Jaquan never showed up, I decided to name him John. Now that my son was born and my father named him John Davis, anger burned in my soul because, once again, my father had to control some part of my life. I had to out figure to add the name I wanted to my son's name without my father knowing. I had lost so much blood during the birth that I lay lifeless and asleep, recovering as my father named my son without my permission. But now, my parents had left, and I saw the opportunity to add to my son's name.

It was time for the nurse to do her rounds, and I asked if I could add my son's name. The registrar said yes, but I could not remove the names on the birth certificate. I said that was fine and then explained to her the name I wanted on the birth certificate, John Lamont Davis Adams.

A few minutes later, my room phone rang. I answered it and heard Jaquan's voice on the other side of the line. He told me he was trying to find a ride to see me and asked how much longer I would be in the hospital. I started to cry.

"Why did you leave me?" I sobbed into the phone.

There was dead silence on the phone for a couple of seconds. I then repeated the question. Jaquan finally spoke, asking again how much longer I would be at the hospital. I told him I would only be there for two more days. I also told him that our son had his last name because he was not there to sign the birth certificate.

Jaquan started to flip out, "How? Who says? That is impossible!"

"My father put his last name on the certificate, so that meant that I could put yours as well."

Jaquan asked me what the baby's name was. When I told him it was John Lamont Davis Adams, the next thing I heard was a dial tone. That was the last time I ever heard from Jaquan. *What is a girl who is 20 years old with a baby supposed to do?* I wondered. After that, I lost contact with Jaquan. Everyone in my family could not believe I had given my son another man's last name, especially a man who was not the child's father.

"You need to call Kenny," they insisted, but I refused. *I would rather die than ever speak to Kenny again,* I thought.

What my family did not know was that a few months before Kenny stopped speaking to me, I went to the doctor and found out that I had contracted an STD. It was chlamydia. I had never in my life had any STDs. Kenny had given me this disease and then had the audacity to come to my school with my supposed friend Stacy and act like I was nothing. That was the reason I lost it. If I had told my family what really happened between Kenny and me, my uncles would have lost it, gone off, and beat him. My family did not need to know that Kenny had burned me and was sleeping with my friends.

CHAPTER 11

YOU WITHOUT JESUS

When you experience a trial, storm, or struggle, the natural reaction is to push all your hurt, pain, frustration, and guilt deep down and make it look like you are doing fine. You think, *This is as good as it is going to be.*

For me, this was the beginning of the bleeding in my own life and over others, just like the woman with the blood situation mentioned in the Bible, which we will talk about later. I wasn't bleeding physically, but I'm talking about when you are dealing with so much in your life that you can't keep it hidden anymore. You can't keep a mask on, pretending that your life is going well when you know everything will fall apart at any moment. The pieces cannot be put back together without hurting the people you love or are close to. This is when you start to lose relationships with family and friends. Bridges start burning up because everything that has happened in your life cannot stay pushed down. Your life is becoming overwhelming to the point where you can't handle it anymore.

You start off fine because your focus is on something, or for me, someone else, rather than the pile of junk in my life. My family was treating me differently because of John, and I felt that my life had changed for the better. I was showing everyone how capable I was by being the woman no one thought I could be, just like a drug addict or an alcoholic who stopped using because they moved to a new town, city, state, or country. For me, I would stop prostituting for a time because I was able to get a job and act like a functioning person. This wasn't my first rodeo or time acting as I knew I wouldn't be acting for any length of time. It was temporary, and I could handle the shortness of the affair.

But all the while, whatever you have pushed down is eating at you. No matter what you do, you forget about it or pretend it never exists because you don't want to deal with the pain when someone or something happens. It sends you off into the deep end. The cycle repeats itself. How many people do you know who may be dealing with drugs, alcohol, porn, manipulating, or gambling and are going through these cycles again? When you realize no matter if you change the place, job, or people around your problems will stay the same. If you have not changed, everything that has and may be happening in your life will eventually lead you back to what you left behind. That is because we are broken and sick, needing a doctor to fix our heart, mind, and soul.

Jesus Christ is called "Jehovah Rapha," the healer. What does that mean? Let's say you were in an accident and broke your leg. You get taken to the hospital to see how bad your leg is. The doctor comes in and says they need to do an x-ray to fully understand what they are dealing with. Some people don't want the x-ray to be done and say, "I'm good," walking out in pain, not knowing what damage has been done. Then some will get an x-ray and see their leg broken in three different places. The doctor then says they can snap it back into place for a temporary fix to get you into surgery. However, you are willing to only allow the doctor to snap it back into place and then walk out, not wanting the surgery to be done. So, now you are walking around with a leg that is painful every time you take a step to the point that all you can do is cry when you walk. So, you get a wheelchair so you can get around, but there are places where you need people to help you get in because you can't walk up some stairs or get through a door.

Jesus Christ is called "Jehovah Rapha," the healer.

You know it's getting worse, but you can't humble yourself to get the proper help to get out of pain, so you start to hurt people around you who are trying to help you. The reason why you are attacking the people around you is that you're mad at yourself for getting to the point where you are dependent on others. You not only inflict pain on other people but also turn on yourself and start hurting yourself because you don't want surgery. But, to get the surgery, you must go through the prep part. That is the consultation with the nurse about your history, where you will have to expose that you may have a heart condition, a family history of cancer, or diabetes. Maybe that is hard to speak about because you have never discussed your history with anyone. You have put up a wall and don't want anyone to know the true pain you are carrying inside. So, you would rather go through this life in extreme pain and die than have the surgery.

Honestly, I have done this my whole life. Even now, there are people in so much pain that they are unwilling to undergo surgery. You look around this nation and see the men and women changing their bodies, and once they do, I know people who wish they never did, and now they are in more pain than ever. Or, because of the pain from the opposite sex, you say that the same gender understands me, but you still have that pain. My father told me the only way I would be married was in a pimp-and-hoe relationship since no men wanted me or understood me. I was in a same-sex relationship because I was one of the people saying the same gender understood me. To other hurting people, it makes sense because of the abuse and pain I went through with my pimps. But I was still hurting. You have people killing people of the same nationality and yet want to say, "life matters" and "Our body. Our choice." Every person in this world is hurting, even Christians. What makes one person different from another is how much they want help to get better.

Some people will say, "No, that is not true because look at my life. Even though I have pain, I'm doing great. I have money, a career, a house, everything, even with this pain, so why do I need to see the doctor for surgery? I have my drinking, drugs, and pornography under control, and I'm not hurting people or bleeding out yet." But this life you are living will not last forever. Either you will break from the pressure of the pain or, like everyone, will one day die, and you will stand before Jesus Christ whether you want to or not, and either Jesus will know you or He won't. But we will get into that later. There is another option: "Choosing rather to suffer affliction with the people of God, than to enjoy the pleasures of sin for a season." (Hebrews 11:25, KJV).

I did not realize that even though I was doing better because of John, I would soon step back into my own hell.

CHAPTER 12

MONEY, MONEY, MONEY

I was doing fairly well for a 20-year-old mom, working as a cashier at Kroger for the past year. I had John in daycare and was doing a great job of saving money toward my own apartment, as I was renting a room in a house for $600 a month. Then, one day my mother called and asked if I could come back home to help them out because my father was sick. John was nine months old, and there were problems at the house where I was staying. In the nine months, the police showed up four times in the apartment. I was uncomfortable raising my son in that environment, so when my mother asked, I didn't wait to answer her.

"Yes," I told my mom, jumping at the chance to get out of that house.

I had about $1,200 saved toward getting an apartment, but my mother shocked me when I returned.

"You have to give me all your savings to help pay the bills," she told me.

"What?" I replied, furious that, once again, my father was using me not because he was sick but because he did not want to work. Meanwhile, I was looking for another job and found one two months later, landing one in the mortgage industry. I was new to the business and was told my commission would be 35 percent when the deal closed, so I took the job. There was one catch.

In the mortgage industry (at least in the company I was in), a person doesn't get paid until they have been there for 90 days. Then, they are paid every two weeks. So, the only way I would get paid during my first 90 days was to build what they call a "pipeline" by making cold calls and getting people to work with me. In 90 days, I was able to get more than 200 individuals to agree to work with me. My first check was for $1,000, the next for $3,500, and the checks just kept coming. I couldn't believe my eyes! I had all this money, would have to file taxes, and felt like I was a productive citizen at age 21.

Then one day, while working on a potentially lucrative loan that would pay me a lot of money, my bosses challenged me to figure out what I would do with the $11,000 I would get. When I mentioned perhaps getting plastic surgery, their mouths dropped.

"Don't you have a kid?" Why not get a car so that you can stop taking public transportation to work?"

"Okay," I replied after thinking about it. "I will look into that."

Two weeks later, I bought a black 2001 Camaro with silver trim, tinted windows, and a leather interior. After I paid for the car, I had it detailed and made sure that the oil was changed and the brakes were done. The first place I took my car to was Terrence's house in Atlanta. Over the past two years, even though I was not speaking to Kenny, that did not stop me from seeing his cousin Terrence, who lived in the same house I had visited when I was in school. The same place where the parties were held.

One day, my friend Denise went riding with John and me. When I pulled up across the street from Terrance's house, I told Denise I would be right back and asked her if she would sit with John while I was gone. I hopped out of the car and ran into the house to see Terrance, who was shocked to see me.

"How did you get here," he asked. "Is John with you?"

"Yes, he's in the car," I replied.

"I'll be right out," he promised.

"No worries, I'll be out by the car waiting," I said as I turned around so fast that I did not hear Terrance trying to tell me something.

As I started running back to the car, I looked down for a split second and ran into someone. It was Kenny. My whole heart stopped.

"Excuse me," he said.

It was Kenny. My whole heart stopped.

I glanced up quickly. "I'm sorry I did not see you, sir," I replied, continuing to walk away while pretending not to know him.

Kenny stopped me and pulled me back towards him. "Riah?" he asked.

"My name is Jean." I retorted sharply.

"Why you acting like this?" he replied.

"Let me go," I said, wanting to get to my car, but he wouldn't let go.

"Is the baby in the car?" he asked.

How did he know I had a baby? I wondered. *The only person that knew about John was Terrance.* Kenny let me go but followed me to my car, quite shocked that I had a Camaro. He pushed me aside and investigated the car. Denise popped up and scared Kenny, making him jump back. Once he realized someone was in the car, he asked her if she would be willing to get out.

"No, she can't," I answered before she could say a word.

Kenny shot me the "if I spoke again there were going to be problems" glare.

I snickered, "That look does not move me anymore. I'm not your girl. Where is Stacy at? Go look at her like that. I don't have time for your games or your sideways looks, acting like you own someone."

As he started stepping my way, I pulled a bat out of my backseat. He stopped dead in his tracks. He then asked if he could see John. I looked at Denise, then back at Kenny. I reluctantly agreed but told him only for one second because John was sleeping, and I did not want him to wake up. Kenny started taking off his shoes and socks.

"What are you doing?" I yelled, "You're going to wake him!"

Kenny turned, looked me straight in the eyes, and said, "This is *my* son, Jean."

"No, it's not," I scoffed. "There's no way that I would ever have your child after how you dismissed me for Stacy and any other girl you want to be with."

Kenny's face changed, and he seemed crushed by what I said. I got in my car and drove off as quickly as possible, knowing I had to get out of there.

CHAPTER 13

EMPTY LOVE

No matter what people say or act like, there is not one person in this world who does not want to be loved by someone. The problem with the word "love" is that it is so loosely used, and people understand its meaning. Yet, it's a word that holds so much power when spoken. Take a second and think about who uses this word. Your parents, siblings, family, friends, boyfriend or girlfriend, your husband, or your wife. How it has been used in your life determines how you look at that simple four-letter word.

It has taken me eight years to start grasping what the word love means. It is defined as "The object of attachment, devotion, or admiration unselfish loyal and benevolent concern for the good of another: such as the fatherly concern of God for humankind, brotherly concern for others."

Before I met Jesus Christ, I had what you call "empty love." I had a love that, when poured into my life, would fall out of life's holes. Think of it as if you had a glass with holes in it so that when you poured water into it, the water leaked out of the holes. That describes the empty love I grew up with and lived in. If you asked my family, they would say they loved me, but unless you have received the pure love of Jesus Christ, such love is conditional. This leads you to start looking and hunting for anyone who will show you the love you think you are looking for. If you don't find it, you may become depressed and desperate over thinking it will never happen to you. Or at least that is what I thought and acted upon.

My home was not the loving, caring home I longed for growing up. When your whole family mentally abuses you by speaking about how you look, belittling you because you are not the smartest person in the family, you start to believe it. People don't understand that parents can either make or break a child to where they start questioning who they are and what they believe. From a young age, I was told that the only thing I would be good at was laying on my back, and if I were to be married, it would be only a pimp-and-hoe relationship. At the end of every conversation, an "I love you" was said to me.

Every time I turned around, there was always a string attached. I had to buy my love all my life. It didn't matter if it was my parents, grandparents, pimps, or so-called friends. If I didn't have money or something to give, they wanted nothing to do with me, or they would make my living situation difficult.

Either I gave in and did what they asked, or they would leave, and I'd be homeless again.

But just like every roller coaster, the ride must end. But when you think you are done with this yo-yo life, you always want to have hope that maybe this time will be different. Everything that has been told to you all your life was a lie, and you will receive the love you see in the romance movies like Princess Bride or Cinderella. When just like anything else, there is no real love. Love is an empty space that pains you when that word is said by the people who hurt you. So, you no longer believe in or feel love. It is to the point that you have created a stone heart with walls up so that you no longer be hurt or used by anyone. This was happening to me.

Before I met Jesus Christ, I had what you call "empty love."

After seeing Kenny, I made it a point to have my walls up and my heart cold towards him, not caring for anyone except John. But what happens when that small piece of you is holding on to hope that this time will be different than any other time? Just like the man in the Bible with the multiple demons called Legion in him.

He cried out for Jesus, as we read about in Mark 5:1-20:

> *"Then they came to the other side of the sea, to the country of the Gadarenes. And when He had come out of the boat, immediately there met Him out of*

the tombs a man with an unclean spirit, who had his dwelling among the tombs; and no one could bind him, not even with chains, because he had often been bound with shackles and chains. And the chains had been pulled apart by him, and the shackles broken in pieces; neither could anyone tame him. And always, night and day, he was in the mountains and in the tombs, crying out and cutting himself with stones. When he saw Jesus from afar, he ran and worshiped Him. And he cried out with a loud voice and said, 'What have I to do with You, Jesus, Son of the Most High God? I implore You by God that You do not torment me.' For He said to him, 'Come out of the man, unclean spirit!' Then He asked him, 'What is your name?' And he answered, saying, 'My name is Legion; for we are many.' Also he begged Him earnestly that He would not send them out of the country. Now a large herd of swine was feeding there near the mountains. So all the demons begged Him, saying, 'Send us to the swine, that we may enter them.' And at once Jesus gave them permission. Then the unclean spirits went out and entered the swine (there were about two thousand); and the herd ran violently down the steep place into the sea, and drowned in the sea. So those who fed the swine fled, and they told it in the city and in the country. And they went out to see what it was that had happened. Then they came to Jesus, and saw the one who had

> *been demon-possessed and had the legion, sitting and clothed and in his right mind. And they were afraid. And those who saw it told them how it happened to him who had been demon-possessed, and about the swine. Then they began to plead with Him to depart from their region. And when He got into the boat, he who had been demon-possessed begged Him that he might be with Him. However, Jesus did not permit him, but said to him, 'Go home to your friends, and tell them what great things the Lord has done for you, and how He has had compassion on you.' And he departed and began to proclaim in Decapolis all that Jesus had done for him; and all marveled." (NKJV)*

What do you do when what you think you want to hear comes true? Do you believe it, or do you stay true to yourself even when you don't know who you really are?

I was about to find out.

CHAPTER 14

MARCUS AND THE WAFFLE HOUSE

Early one morning, I met a guy at the Waffle House and began hanging out with him. Marcus was 24, about 5'9", and heavy into cocaine to the point where his nose would bleed, and he could not stop it. I also started doing cocaine to stay awake for work because Marcus had convinced me that we were boyfriend and girlfriend. He showed me love like no one ever had, and I felt like I was the only girl he wanted to be with. It was to the point where I introduced Marcus to my parents because he made me feel like "the only one."

One afternoon, Marcus and I sat on the couch when he leaned over. "How much do you love me?" he asked. "Would you do anything for me?"

"You are my heart," I replied. "Whatever you want, daddy," using the expression girls use to address their pimp.

We had been seeing each other for almost two months, and it was getting to the point that when his boys showed up at the crib, I would have to answer him with, "Yes, daddy," or "What would you like, daddy?" Then, suddenly, he asked, "Can you sleep with a friend of mine so we can get some coke?" Once again, I wanted to be loved by a man so badly that I agreed to do it. I was put right back in that mindset of becoming numb to my reality that I was not being truly loved by a man. The lies were getting louder in my head about how I was not what a man wanted around them unless I could provide for his gain, no matter how I felt. The next thing I knew, I was back doing the same thing I had just gotten out of eight months ago.

One day, Marcus called me saying that he needed three hundred dollars. "Give me a couple of hours, and the money will be behind my car license plate," I told him, lying through my teeth. "You can pick it up at 8:00," I continued, knowing I was going to ignore his request. After blowing him off, he began calling me, but I ignored his calls, thinking and hoping he would stop calling. He did stop but instead showed up at my parent's house looking for me.

"There is someone here to see you," my father called out. I came out of my room, went to the door, and my heart dropped into my stomach.

Marcus asked if I could step outside to talk with him. I did so but left my door cracked a bit so that if anything happened, I could run back inside.

"Why aren't you answering your phone, and where is my money?" He asked me. I told him it was behind the license plate, and he said it wasn't because he had already checked.

Once again, I wanted to be loved by a man so badly that I agreed to do it.

"If you don't have the money, I'm leaving you because you're useless to me, and you must not love me," he added. Then, he pushed me and walked away.

My father saw it, came out, and got in Marcus' face. Crying, I ran back into the house, put my shoes on, and tried to run out. I couldn't let the man who said he loved me walk out of my life.

My father stopped, picked me up, and brought me back into the house.

"What is wrong with you, and why are you chasing after a man that just put his hands on you?"

"I don't know," I meekly replied. *Maybe it's because I had a father who always beat me and then said, "I love you,"* I thought.

I went crying into my mother's room. My mom rubbed my hair and told me I could do better than that, and I fell asleep on her lap. I was startled by my father later that night when he said Marcus was calling and threatening us, but no one took him seriously. After that night, I never saw Marcus again.

One sunny afternoon while my father was in his office working, he called me in to talk about what my future was going to look like. Again, I never thought about what I would do next after returning home.

> *"You can't continue living in my house if you don't have a plan," he told me, suggesting I attend college. He had made it clear he was not happy that I listened to my mother and took a year off from school after graduating high school. So, once again, as a lost puppy looking for love and approval, I reluctantly agreed to attend a junior college to please my father.*

I hated school because anything having to do with learning was not my cup of tea. My father and other family members had always told me I was not smart enough, but my father said it was either college or going back on the streets. This was my last chance for my parents to help me before I completely burned that bridge. So, as any wise person would do, I chose college.

CHAPTER 15

SNOWING IN GEORGIA

I didn't see Kenny for about another year. Then, one day while working as a bank teller for Citizens Trust Bank, I heard this deep voice that sent a shiver down my spine. I looked up, and Kenny was standing right in front of me. He started with the normal charm he employs when he wants a woman.

"You look beautiful today. You work here now? When do you get off? Can I take you out for dinner?" he asked, peppering me with multiple questions.

I wanted to say, "Hell Nah! I want nothing to do with you, Kenny." But before I could respond, he touched my hand.

"I miss you. I need to see you. Please have dinner with me," he pleaded.

"Why? Where are your other girlfriends? Why do you miss me? What's wrong now? All the other girls have come to realize how pathetic you really are?"

Kenny leaned over and said, "You don't mean any of that. You seem hurt and mad at me. Ever since I saw you and your boy, I haven't been able to get you out of my head."

"You could have called. I have a phone. It has been a year since I saw you last, and I know you got my number from Terrance, so don't stand here and make it seem like I have been on your mind. Now, if you don't mind, I have other customers that need my attention."

He took a deep breath, and tears started streaming down his face. "I need you, Jean," He whispered.

I couldn't resist him as he held my hand. The way he looked into my eyes, the sweet smell of his cologne, and his soft touch made me feel like things would be different this time. I agreed to have dinner with him that night. Before returning to business, I took a deep breath and asked him if he had an account with us and needed to conduct any transactions. Kenny chuckled and told me he was only there to see me and ask me out. I smiled and sternly said that if he called me after nine o'clock, I was not going anywhere with him.

After I was through with my shift, I went home to shower and change. I called my girlfriend Amber, my son's God auntie, to see if she would watch him for me while I went on a date. She was initially reluctant because she hated Kenny (after I told her everything he had done to me). Still, after a minute of convincing, she agreed to watch him for the night.

When I got there, Amber told me that John had to be asleep before I left, and if he woke up while I was gone, I would need to return to her house right away. I agreed and told her that I would shoot a few bills her way for watching him. I finished dressing and got John to settle down for me so I could leave him. I was astounded when my phone rang just before nine o'clock. When I answered, I heard the sexiest, deepest voice on the other end. I had forgotten what Kenny sounded like on the phone. I told him I was taken aback that he really did what he said he would do.

"Can you pick me up at my cousin's house?" he asked.

I almost said no but instead told him, "I will call you when I am on the block, but if you're not outside when I pull up, I'm not waiting around."

I got in my car, drove to Terrance's, and Kenny stood outside waiting. When he got in the car, he looked at me and asked if I wanted to forget dinner.

"Let's just go somewhere to have some fun with the two of us," he suggested.

"Sure," I replied, which is when Kenny told me to switch sides and let him drive.

"Are you interested in losing the baby fat from being pregnant with John?" he asked while driving.

Wanting to do anything to keep him and eventually become his wife, I said "Yes," although he did not tell me how I could lose the weight. Only that he was going to make sure the weight was gone.

When we got to Motel 6 in Tucker, Georgia, Kenny just looked at me.

"I need money to get a room," he said.

That should have been a red flag for me, as it would have been for anyone else. But I was so desperate for Kenny to touch me that I gave him the money for the room. When we got inside, Kenny said, "Let's get turnt up," gave me a fifth of Henn, and said, "Crack it." I stood there for a moment, shaking my head, when he came up close to me, grabbed me by my waist, started kissing my neck and lips, and did his famous whisper in my ear. Then, he said the three words I have wanted to hear from him since the day I met him.

"I love you."

That should have been a red flag for me.

The next line that Kenny dropped on me after we kissed for a good two or three minutes sealed the deal for me to do anything and everything for him. "You know that John is my baby, and we will be together."

Oh, how those words would forever scar me to my soul as I began drinking the Hennessey. The next thing I knew, Kenny pulled a Ziplock bag out of his pocket with some white stuff in it.

"What is that? I asked, having never seen anything like it. It was crack. Then, he pulled out some coke from his other pocket.

When I saw the coke, all I could think of was Marcus. There was no way out of this situation, and Kenny knew it. He told me this would help me lose weight, and if I loved him, I would do it with him. So, that night I did about fifteen lines and smoked some crack. I wanted to make love to Kenny, but he was more concerned with getting more coke. At one point, he took my car and left me at the motel for almost three hours. I panicked, called him more than a dozen times, and got no response. So, the next best thing I thought I needed to do was call the police because I did not know what had happened to Kenny or my car.

As I was about to call the police, Kenny returned with my car. I lost it and started hitting him and yelling at him.

"How could he leave me there by myself for that long?" I screamed. I grabbed my keys and started to walk out of the room when he seized me and slammed the door.

"You're not going anywhere."

"Like hell I'm not!" I screamed, "You left me and didn't answer my calls. Do you know that I almost called the police because I didn't know where you were, and you had my car?"

Kenny politely reminded me that I was in a room full of drugs and that if I had called the police, I would have gone to jail.

I stood there and shook my head. "I'm so good off of you, Kenny. You still playing those stupid games."

He started kissing me on the lips passionately, making me feel like I was important to him. It was the first time he had ever done that. He whispered in my ear that he loved me and wanted to ensure we had everything we needed for the night. I told him it was already three o'clock in the morning, and I needed to get back to Amber's house by eight to get John.

He had me lick my finger, stick it in the bag of coke, and put it in my mouth. My mouth was getting a numbing feeling that I had never experienced before in my life. Although we had sex, we were both high, and I honestly didn't feel anything afterward. We left the motel that morning around seven o'clock to get back to Denise's house before John woke up.

I called her when I was almost to the house and asked if Kenny could come inside to use the bathroom while I grabbed John. Amber was not fond of Kenny being in her house, but since we were almost there, she said it was fine. When we walked in, I went to get John ready to go home when I heard gunshots and screaming coming from the back. I quickly put John back down in the playpen to see what was going on. That is when I saw Kenny pinned against the wall with a gun pointed at his head.

Amber's husband had found Kenny doing lines of coke on the nightstand in their bedroom, and she was trying to talk her husband down while yelling at me for bringing Kenny into her house. Amber started coming at me like she wanted to fight and threw a jab at me, but I caught her hand. I told her I did not know what Kenny was doing and asked, "Would I have brought him in if I knew?"

She told me never to ever come back. I started crying because she was like my sister. I told Kenny to come on, and Amber's husband told him not to say a word, or he would shoot him for what he had done in his house.

I went into the room to get John and pick up my stuff to leave. Kenny went to the car, and as I walked out of the house, Amber came up behind me and helped me carry John's bag. She said that I needed to lay low for a minute before returning to her house and that if I ever came back, I was never to bring Kenny with me. I apologized to her and said that this would never happen again.

Then, I got into the car and glared at Kenny. He looked at me and said, "What?" He acted as if nothing happened and said I should not be trippin' off something like that. I told him that I wanted nothing to do with him and that he was never to call me again.

CHAPTER 16

FEELING UNWANTED AND NOT ENOUGH

Who doesn't want to feel accepted by people? Whether by family, friends, colleagues, peers at school, or even at your church. No one in this world says they don't desire to be wanted by someone. Everyone goes on a quest to find love. For some, their identity is based upon what social media displays with wanting to be with someone. For others, it becomes a mission to fulfill so you're not looked upon as if no one wants you. That may mean putting yourself in situations you know are dangerous and/or toxic. People are so desperate in that longing that they will do anything to obtain it. So, for me, I became a prostitute.

But what happens when you do everything you can to be wanted, fit in, and prove to people that they should accept you, only to end up with a broken heart, abused, and being told you are damaged goods? You don't have to be a prostitute like I was to understand the feeling of being rejected. It can happen to anyone.

For example, a woman named Leah experienced the feeling of being unwanted by both her father and then her husband. Who is this woman, Leah? She was Laban's older daughter and one of Jacob's two wives. She was also the mother of Judah and in the lineage of Jesus Christ. Sounds like a great life with everything going well, right? Unless you know what is going on in someone else's life, you will be deceived. Today, we call that putting on a front, having a smoke screen up, or showing two faces.

So, when I read her story in Genesis 29, I ask, "Why was Jesus born through Leah's lineage and not Rachel's (the other wife)?"

> *"So Jacob went on his journey and came to the land of the people of the East. And he looked, and saw a well in the field; and behold, there were three flocks of sheep lying by it; for out of that well they watered the flocks. A large stone was on the well's mouth. Now all the flocks would be gathered there; and they would roll the stone from the well's mouth, water the sheep, and put the stone back in its place on the well's mouth. And Jacob said to them, 'My brethren, where are you from?' And they said, 'We are from Haran.' Then he said to them, 'Do you know Laban the son of Nahor?' And they said,*

'We know him.' So he said to them, 'Is he well?' And they said, 'He is well. And look, his daughter Rachel is coming with the sheep.' Then he said, 'Look, it is still high day; it is not time for the cattle to be gathered together. Water the sheep, and go and feed them.' But they said, 'We cannot until all the flocks are gathered together, and they have rolled the stone from the well's mouth; then we water the sheep.' Now while he was still speaking with them, Rachel came with her father's sheep, for she was a shepherdess. And it came to pass, when Jacob saw Rachel the daughter of Laban his mother's brother, and the sheep of Laban his mother's brother, that Jacob went near and rolled the stone from the well's mouth, and watered the flock of Laban his mother's brother. Then Jacob kissed Rachel, and lifted up his voice and wept. And Jacob told Rachel that he was her father's relative and that he was Rebekah's son. So she ran and told her father. Then it came to pass, when Laban heard the report about Jacob his sister's son, that he ran to meet him, and embraced him and kissed him, and brought him to his house. So he told Laban all these things. And Laban said to him, 'Surely you are my bone and my flesh.' And he stayed with him for a month. Then Laban said to Jacob, 'Because you are my relative, should you therefore serve me for nothing? Tell me, what should your wages be?' Now Laban had two daughters: the name of the elder was Leah, and the name of

the younger was Rachel. Leah's eyes were delicate, but Rachel was beautiful of form and appearance. Now Jacob loved Rachel; so he said, 'I will serve you seven years for Rachel your younger daughter.' And Laban said, 'It is better that I give her to you than that I should give her to another man. Stay with me.' So Jacob served seven years for Rachel, and they seemed only a few days to him because of the love he had for her. Then Jacob said to Laban, 'Give me my wife, for my days are fulfilled, that I may go in to her.' And Laban gathered together all the men of the place and made a feast. Now it came to pass in the evening, that he took Leah his daughter and brought her to Jacob; and he went in to her. And Laban gave his maid Zilpah to his daughter Leah as a maid. So it came to pass in the morning, that behold, it was Leah. And he said to Laban, 'What is this you have done to me? Was it not for Rachel that I served you? Why then have you deceived me?' And Laban said, 'It must not be done so in our country, to give the younger before the firstborn. Fulfill her week, and we will give you this one also for the service which you will serve with me still another seven years.' Then Jacob did so and fulfilled her week. So he gave him his daughter Rachel as wife also. And Laban gave his maid Bilhah to his daughter Rachel as a maid. Then Jacob also went in to Rachel, and he also loved Rachel more than Leah. And he served with

> *Laban still another seven years. When the Lord saw that Leah was unloved, He opened her womb; but Rachel was barren. So Leah conceived and bore a son, and she called his name Reuben; for she said, 'The Lord has surely looked on my affliction. Now therefore, my husband will love me.' Then she conceived again and bore a son, and said, 'Because the Lord has heard that I am unloved, He has therefore given me this son also.' And she called his name Simeon. She conceived again and bore a son, and said, 'Now this time my husband will become attached to me, because I have borne him three sons.' Therefore his name was called Levi. And she conceived again and bore a son, and said, 'Now I will praise the Lord.' Therefore she called his name Judah. Then she stopped bearing." (Genesis 29:1-35, NKJV)*

Jacob wanted Rachel because of her beauty, but because Leah was not as beautiful as Rachel. Laban deceived Jacob. Jacob should not have been mad at Laban because many times Jacob had deceived people. Jacob had deceived his brother for the birthright and then deceived his father, Isaac, in receiving the blessing. So, the deceiver was himself deceived and shocked that Jacob slept with Leah instead of Rachel and had to work seven more years for Rachel would like anyone mad.

> All my life, I have wanted to be loved and accepted by people.

Did you see in Leah's story that she did everything possible to be wanted by her husband, yet it was not good enough? All my life, I have wanted to be loved and accepted by people, even after becoming a Christian. I thought that if I did things for people, they would love me or at least like me more. However, it has been just recently I have learned that I will never be able to please people.

Referring to Jesus, John writes about this in John 2:23-25:

> *"Now when He was in Jerusalem at the Passover, during the feast, many believed in His name when they saw the signs which He did. But Jesus did not commit Himself to them, because He knew all men, and had no need that anyone should testify of man, for He knew what was in man." (NKJV)*

So, approval from man will never come. There will always be something the person you are looking to get approval from finds wrong with you to not accept you. I thought that if I got the most money and did everything I could to make my pimps happy, I would one day be their wife. Or, if I showed them I was loyal and down for them, I would be loved and wanted.

But, just like Leah, who the Lord saw was unloved, in the same way, Jesus saw me in my pit of darkness. After all the money and sex I did for years, I was considered damaged goods. If you don't know Jesus, you don't know that He welcomes and loves those the world discards as human waste. When people don't want anything to do with you, Jesus comes into your life and transforms you into what the Scriptures say:

> *"But God hath chosen the foolish things of the world to confound the wise; and God hath chosen the weak things of the world to confound the things which are mighty." (1 Corinthians 1:27, KJV)*

God had His promised seed come through the lineage of Judah, so Jesus Christ is called the Lion of Judah. The last eight years of my life have been more than I could ever imagine. The love and acceptance of Jesus are more than I could ever imagine. To know that Jesus Christ calls me by name and is not ashamed of me to the point where I am His daughter that he takes care of. We will talk more about that later.

If you feel unloved, unaccepted, and unwanted and that your life is falling apart, whether visible to people or not, know that Jesus sees you. He wants to come into your life and show you true love and acceptance.

CHAPTER 17

THE ROCK

"I want nothing to do with you, and don't ever call me again," I told Kenny.

There was a long silence in the car before he spoke. "There are things you need to do if you want me out of your life," he replied.

I looked at him and smirked as I pulled up to Terrence's house.

"I will need $2,000 before I leave you alone, or you will be brutalized by some men," he continued before stepping out of the car.

"When do you need the money?" I asked. "I will wire it to you, so I don't have to see you," I replied.

"You have until Saturday," he replied, giving me only three days.

That night I went online and posted an ad, jumping back into the nightmare of prostitution that I was so desperate to escape. For the next few days, I would sneak out of my parent's house to meet up with my "dates." In no time, I had made $3,500. When Saturday arrived, I got a phone call from Kenny.

"Where do you want me to send the money?" I asked before he could say a word. "I am going to Western Union the money to you, and then I want you to never call me again."

He was dumbfounded, thinking I could never come up with that kind of money so quickly. "Where did you get the money from?" he asked.

"Not your concern," was my terse reply, "You have no control over me, and I'm done with you."

"If that's what you want, then fine, I'm done with you too," Kenny responded, telling me where to send the money. So, I drove to a Western Union store and wired the money, texting Kenny the ten-digit number. I was so glad that chapter in my life was done. At least, that's what I thought at the time.

Kenny did not know that the day I ran into him at Terrance's house, I met a man named Malik. He knew everything about Kenny and me because he lived a block down from Terrance's house, and I would see him when I came over to see Terrance. After the conversation with Kenny, a few weeks went by, and I started feeling good about myself again. I didn't have to worry about Kenny or being a hoe to get some money for a man. Occasionally, I would speak to Malik when he called, but I wasn't looking at my phone every second of the day to see if he would call me. Instead, I would go about my day, and if he called, great. If not, it was no sweat off my back.

I became so confident in myself that I wasn't concerned about hooking back up with Kenny after running into him one day at a store. When Kenny saw me in the store, I was reminded why I was no longer with him. I remembered how he could sometimes be aggressive and demanding in receiving information. Kenny had approached me wanting to know why I was dealing with Malik and warning me the stay away from Malik, or I would be in trouble. I dismissed his threat and started to walk away when Kenny grabbed my arm so tight it was bruising. I knew the only way Kenny would let me go was if I agreed to his order. At that moment, I agreed, but I wanted to be with a man who had never put his hands on me. The only man I could think of at that moment was Malik.

I tried calling Malik, and when he answered the phone, I heard the smooth, refreshing tone in his voice. The longer we stayed on the phone, the more Malik was intrigued about seeing and getting to know me. He suggested I meet him the next day, and I happily agreed. However, he wanted to meet at night, which I was reluctant to agree to because that meant lying and sneaking out of my parent's house again and leaving John for my parents to watch. But that is precisely what I did the next night. I waited for John to fall asleep and my father to finally go to bed when I snuck out of the house. Then, I drove to Terrance's block on the Westside of Atlanta, where Malik lived.

When I got to a familiar corner, I turned off the engine and called Malik to see if I could kick it with him. The phone rang and rang, but there was no answer. So, I tried one last time.

Finally, Malik answered his phone. He sounded baffled about why I was calling him because it was so late. I told him that I was on his block and wanted to know if I could see him. He told me to get off his block, to never call him, and he would call me when he was ready to see me.

After talking to him, my car wouldn't start. Then, suddenly, my phone rang. It was Teddy, a guy I met at a club one night. I told him what had just happened and asked him where he was and if he would be willing to pick me up. Teddy wasn't driving and was with one of his boys. I told him that was fine. I just needed to get out of there. When I told him where I was, he was not happy but agreed to come and get me. I told him I would pay him back.

"Oh yeah, you are going to owe me tonight," he replied.

I had no idea what that meant, so I replied, "Sure, whatever it takes." But then, I heard his friend say in the background that they would be there in about twenty minutes or so.

I had locked my doors while waiting in my car when suddenly I heard a woman screaming. The next thing I knew, someone was banging on my passenger window. It was the woman I heard screaming. She begged me to let her in my car, but I saw a man with a gun just as I was about to unlock the doors.

"If you let her in, I will kill you," he said.

I was scared and just covered my eyes, praying for someone to save me. The next thing I heard was the man yelling at the woman to hurry up because he thought the police were coming. My phone rang. Teddy said they were there and to hurry up and get in. I quickly grabbed my purse and keys, jumped out of my car, and ran into theirs.

"If you let her in, I will kill you," he said.

"Do you know those people?" they asked me once I got in.

"No," I replied, thanking them for getting me on such short notice.

"No problem," they assured me.

We drove for a cool minute when they pulled up to a house that looked abandoned.

"Get out of the car," they told me.

"Whose house is this," I asked, "and why are we here?"

They didn't respond, repeating that I needed to get out and start walking. Once we made it to the house, a man knocked me to the ground, and the other man ripped my clothes off. I screamed and cried while being raped. Finally, I fought my way out of the house. Then, they pulled their guns out and started shooting at me as I ran.

I finally got to a familiar street and started walking back to my car. By now, it was about seven thirty in the morning. I called Denise and was surprised when she answered. I told her what had happened and asked for her help. About thirty minutes later, her brother-in-law showed up. He looked to see what was wrong with the car, then took me to AutoZone to pick up the part I needed. We went back to my car, and he began working on it. After he finished fixing the car, it started right up. I thanked him and paid him with the sixty dollars I had in my car.

Before I drove away, Amber pulled up to the driveway blocking me in. I turned my car off and started to cry. Amber came to my door and opened it. She reached in to hug me and said, "It's going to be okay." Amber then asked why I didn't call her the minute my car wasn't starting.

"I wasn't going to call you because I thought you were still mad at me for what had happened with Kenny," I told her. She said to call her if something like that ever happened again.

"Thanks," I replied. "That means a lot."

As I began pulling out of the driveway, my phone rang. It was my mother. I couldn't answer it. So, I drove back to my parents' house, parked my car, and walked inside. My father told me that I was not allowed to live there anymore, I could not take John, and if I tried to leave with him, they would call the police. That night I went into the living room, sat next to my son, and held him tightly. I was crying profusely because I didn't want to let him go.

"I love you more than life itself, and you are my heart, always," I told him, adding that mommy had to go and that I would be back for him soon.

"Mommy, don't cry, don't cry. Mommy, why are you crying?" he asked, looking at me.

I could only say that papa and grandma would take care of him but that I would be back. I hugged my son again as if it would be the last time I would ever see him.

After that, I walked out of my son's life and found shelter for the night. I called Kenny to see if he could get me out of there.

"For a fee," he replied.

"How much?" I asked, and of course, it was a crazy number that he wanted in only a couple of hours. I was able to get the money and meet him in Roswell. When he got in the car, he did not look the same as the last time I saw him. He told me to drive, and soon we ended up in Stone Mountain, Georgia.

The house he took me to looked okay, but there was smoke everywhere when I walked in. I did not know what I was getting myself into until Kenny told me to sit on the couch and not speak. I was beside myself and could not believe I was in a crack house. I thought those houses only existed in movies like "New Jack City," but not in real life. Let alone not in my reality. A few minutes later, Kenny returned with some white crystals in his hand. "Try it."

"What is it?" I asked with a puzzled look on my face.

He slapped me in the face. "Don't ask questions. Just do it."

He handed me a lighter and something to smoke on. The next thing I knew, I was high, off something, but I didn't know what. I couldn't sit still. Finally, a woman walked into the room and said, "that was some good crystal!"

I looked at Kenny, "I…I just smoked…meth."

"You act like you never had that before."

"No, I haven't. I don't do that stuff."

"You do now!" The woman laughed.

I spent months living in that dope house with Kenny, going out on dates to make money so I could live there and stay high. Then one day, while returning from a date, I saw the police raiding the house. So, I asked the guy I was with if he could take me to the closest motel. He brought me to a rundown motel that only cost $70 a night. I had enough money for four nights but had no clothes except the ones on my back. So, when I finally made it into the room, I showered and sat down to figure out what my next step would be.

I called one of my dates to see if they would take me shopping for some clothes and told him that could be his payment for me. After he left my room, I received a phone call. I answered it, and the voice on the other end was a recording.

"This is a collect call from Kenny at the county jail. To accept this call, press one, and to decline press two," it said.

I pressed two. I was done with Kenny.

CHAPTER 18

LOST IN ASHES

In my world of sex, drugs, and violence, my small light of hope and love left me when I had to walk out of John's life. All I saw was darkness, every moment alone in this cold, dark world. It was as if my breath had been taken from me.

No one in my family wanted to be connected to me because of my street reputation. There were countless times of being raped. Sinking myself into drugs, hoping I would die because there was no point in living anymore. Having experienced so much violence I couldn't smoke weed and would have a panic attack if forced to do so. I was just like Mary of Magdalen, who no one in the Jewish culture wanted to have anything to do with.

Crystal meth was now my new best friend. It would numb my body, so I did not have to feel anything. I became a walking dead person. Meth wasn't just opening me up to being brutally beaten every day, but it allowed demons into my soul. If you don't think demons or the devil are real, do not be deceived. They are as real as you and I. Mary of Magdalen—whom many believe was a prostitute—was also plagued by demons.

We read about her in Luke 8:1-3:

> *"Now it came to pass, afterward, that He went through every city and village, preaching and bringing the glad tidings of the kingdom of God. And the twelve were with Him, and certain women who had been healed of evil spirits and infirmities—Mary called Magdalene, out of whom had come seven demons." (NKJV)*

Just like Mary of Magdalen was tormented by evil spirits, so was I for many years. I was used like merchandise, leaving me not knowing my identity. I believed the false narratives others told me about myself. No man would want to marry or be with a woman with my background. So, I became involved in relationships with either a Madam (a woman pimp) or with women that were bi-sexual or lesbians. All because I thought I could be accepted and loved by them.

But it didn't work, and the lies that played in my mind started returning. Lies that I would never be good enough for marriage if I did give up everything about who I was to get what I had always wanted, such as being a wife with a family. Instead, I kept going deeper into the darkness, lost in my ashes.

Every day I forced myself to believe that if a man didn't love me, then a woman would because that is what I was good for. However, that didn't come true, so I got mad and determined that someone was going to love me. I was doing everything and anything that would show I was a woman a man would want to have as a wife. And, when the lies came back into my mind, I would smoke more meth and be willing to do other drugs to make the voices in my head dull and silent for a time. I would get so high that I couldn't perform for my pimps. As a result of not reaching my quota, I would receive punishments from my pimps that would end up with me staring at a gun in my face or being tortured by them.

It was a cycle that went on for years. Finally, it got to the point that I realized that my pimps would never be with me because they all had wives already.

So, like any other time, I left my last pimp and went to a different state, where I prostituted to get a motel room and drugs. I tried to kill myself by smoking as many drugs as possible. Still, I realized I did whatever those men said to prove my love to them, only to be left alone in a motel room. Still, I was nothing but ashes. I was skinnier than ever, but I kept seeing my stomach getting big, so I did more drugs because I had to stay skinny if I wanted more money.

Then one day, I was once again homeless with no money or a roof over my head. I had pimps that made me sleep on sidewalks, under the freeway in a hole, in a tent on a beach, and in bathrooms because I didn't make my quota. So, I went to the hospital for shelter. I told them that my stomach was hurting, and I was told I was pregnant. I didn't believe the doctor because, for the past decade, I had been told I could not have children because of the many surgeries I had undergone to remove cysts on my ovaries. After leaving the hospital, I called my former pimp and told him I was pregnant with his baby.

"Where is my $1,500 that you are supposed to wire me at?" was his only response. I started crying.

"You didn't hear me. I am having your baby."

He told me not to say that and to be quiet. Then, he said I was lying because I didn't want to send him the money.

At that moment, something clicked in me. *I am done with this man and life,* I thought. I cried out to God. I was tired of bleeding all over the United States. I was not physically bleeding; however, I was carrying around all my problems and baggage. I thought I could start fresh, not realizing until I allowed Jesus to come into my life that none of life's lies and baggage would go away. I wanted to change my life. I knew if I didn't get help, I was going to die.

But, as usual, when you leave your pimps, they do what any taskmaster does: retrieve their slave. They put fear in you that if you don't come back and give them their money, you will lose your life, or, in my case, the people close to me would lose their lives. They put fear in you that if you don't come back and give them their money, you will lose your life, or, in my case, the people close to me would lose their lives.

> I knew in my heart that I would die before ever entering the pit of hell again.

I lived with that fear. I was tired of living in fear of losing my life at any moment. I wanted to be free from the constant demands and abuse of the dark world. I didn't know what being free looked like or how I would obtain the freedom I was now searching for. But I was determined to find and have it. No matter what I had to do, I knew in my heart that I would die before ever entering the pit of hell again.

At the moment, I didn't realize how much fight it would take to have the freedom I was seeking and to get out of the grip of darkness and death. Just taking the first step was so hard. The emergency shelter allowed you to stay there for 45 days. After that, you had to find another place. The shelter's director informed me that I was running out of time, and I knew that my pimps were still looking for me. So I needed to find a place so I would not be found.

I had called 27 domestic shelters that told me no, I couldn't come because my situation was too severe and one that would put other women's lives in danger. I could only cry as I begged these places to take me in. It was not in one state that I would call. It was different states around the country that said no. Some would hang up on me when I started crying. Lies would run through my mind that I could not get out, that I needed to go and make it right with my pimps. If I made it right with them, my punishment would not be too bad.

Every day for four straight weeks, as I stayed in the emergency shelter, I would battle back and forth between going back and giving up this fight. But what was I going back to? My family had disowned me and considered me dead to them. And men just used and abused me until I was nothing but trash. I was done folding under pressure from people who did not care about me and wanted nothing except what they could get out of me. These people would not care if I died tomorrow as long as they got what they wanted.

I wanted to be happy even though I didn't understand what that looked or felt like. Not the relief I get to live another day happy. Or the "I'm on drugs, so my emotions and reality are not present, so I can be happy" feeling. I wanted a happiness that I couldn't explain in my life and one that no one could take away. I didn't realize that the whole time I was fighting to get out of my ashes that I was looking for what the Bible says in John 10:10: "The thief cometh not, but for to steal, and to kill, and to destroy: I am come that they might have life, and that they might have it more abundantly." (KJV)

But would I get out of this darkness of "The Game?" I only had fifteen days left to be at the domestic shelter until I had to leave to return to the streets and the life I just ran from. What would you do if you were staring at the fork in the road of your life and it was staring right back at you? How would you handle the voices telling you to return to the life you just left because you know nothing but pain? Not only dealing with being pregnant and trying to figure out if you will keep the baby.

Who will come and save me from the pit I am standing in? I wondered. *Who will rescue me from the death door I know will see if I turn back to the darkness?*

Who indeed.

CHAPTER 19

ISSUE OF BLOOD

You would think getting death threats from men, becoming pregnant before I was 21, being put in a tub full of cold water and ice, and having a gun pointed at my head would stop me from living the way I did. It should have motivated me to change my life and live a peaceful life. But sadly, that was not the case.

I got help from others escaping that last horrifying experience, even moving to a different state, but nothing changed. It was like when I lived with my parents, started school, and headed in the right direction. There was still an emptiness that I could not explain, a longing, and a part of myself missing that I did not understand. This time, though, was different because I was not only in a different state but homeless and did not know a soul.

Now, I'm trying to find my way in this strange state and push my feelings down because I don't have my son with me or a man that loves me. So, I do what I know best. I go looking for ways to get my mind off the pain I was carrying and those feelings of loss and guilt that I didn't know how to express to anyone.

With that mentality, I became easy prey for predators. I found myself being around men like all the others I had dealt with. They started off nice and kind, helping me with money and food. Even though I was living in a shelter and then a recovery house for women dealing with drug issues. But soon, I was around men involved with street life. Suddenly, I was no longer dealing with one or two men but four or five men from different states that needed me to make money. And, of course, the same question came to my mind: *What did I get myself into?*

It reminded me of the woman with the issue of blood, spoken of in the Bible. The woman bled for 12 years and was not allowed to be among the Jewish people. The law in Leviticus explained that during a woman's menstrual impurity, she was unclean, and anything or anyone she touched would be unclean too.

We read about her in Mark 5:25-34:

> *"Now a certain woman had a flow of blood for twelve years, and had suffered many things from many physicians. She had spent all that she had and was no better, but rather grew worse. When she heard about Jesus, she came behind Him in the crowd and touched His garment. For she said, 'If*

> *only I may touch His clothes, I shall be made well.' Immediately the fountain of her blood was dried up, and she felt in her body that she was healed of the affliction. And Jesus, immediately knowing in Himself that power had gone out of Him, turned around in the crowd and said, 'Who touched My clothes?' But His disciples said to Him, 'You see the multitude thronging You, and You say, "Who touched Me?"' And He looked around to see her who had done this thing. But the woman, fearing and trembling, knowing what had happened to her, came and fell down before Him and told Him the whole truth. And He said to her, 'Daughter, your faith has made you well. Go in peace, and be healed of your affliction.'"* (NKJV)

This woman had gone to many different doctors to be freed from this illness, and it was becoming impossible. Think about that for a moment. Imagine having some condition that every doctor and treatment you try doesn't work. What do you think your mental state would be? You would have feelings of hopelessness and desperation, be overwhelmed with anxiety, and be fearful that you will never overcome this disease. You would feel abandoned because people don't want to have anything to do with you because they don't understand why you are in this state. You would feel like Job when he lost his children, his health was gone, and his wife told him to curse God and die.

I became easy prey for predators.

During these moments, Satan comes to kill, steal, and destroy to ensure you never experience the abundant life Jesus gives. But this woman was different. Even though she bled for many years, she didn't give up. Instead, she fought her way through the crowd to see Jesus. Her desperation became determination and faith that he could cure her. She was done with trying everything else given to her, only to end up just like she was before.

Sometimes hurt and suffering never stop flowing. In my case, for the next seven years of my life, I ran around the entire United States, bleeding all over the place. I'd move to a new state, start off great, and then end up right back in the same situation selling my body, doing meth, and dealing with the mental and physical abuse. All the while knowing there was something better than what I was experiencing.

Going back to the Bible story, there came a moment when the woman heard that Jesus was in a nearby city. She pushed through the crowd to touch the hem of Jesus's garment, fighting for her freedom from her bondage. It wasn't the fact that she touched his garment that healed her, but her faith in him. She had heard the stories about him healing the blind, lame, and sick. She knew he would be able to heal her as well.

When dealing with pain, we tend to mask, cover, or try to fix it ourselves, believing we have a handle on it. Until it reverses and that drink, relationship, drug, or addiction takes hold. You can't get away from it. Once again, there must be a breaking point like there was for this woman. A moment where you say, "I'll do everything and anything to be set free."

This only happens when you come to the end of yourself, and every door, opportunity, and bridge around you is gone, closed, and burnt up. Then, the only thing you need and can do is say, "God, please help. I need you. Save me."

I was slowly inching my way toward that moment of surrender.

CHAPTER 20

COLD PATH BACK TO REALITY

A couple of months passed, and I found myself in Los Angeles, standing on a street corner, laughing on the phone. Suddenly, an old woman came up to me.

"You're not allowed to be here, and if you don't leave, I'm going to call the police," she told me.

"Who's that?" my pimp at the time asked me.

"Just some old lady screaming at me."

"I don't know what you're talking about," I began explaining to the woman. "I'm talking on the phone to my husband, who is on his way to pick me up," I continued.

Suddenly, she pepper sprayed me in the eyes.

"Get someone to come help me," I screamed over the phone as I blindly staggered down the street, not knowing where I was going or where I was until I got near a McDonald's. After arriving, I begged the staff to give me something for my eyes, as I was beginning to lose my eyesight. They handed me some milk and led me to the bathroom. After about an hour of pouring milk and water into my eyes, the stinging became bearable. I came out of the bathroom and thanked the people at McDonald's.

I walked out, filled with anger, not knowing what to do with myself.

Knowing in my heart that there was a God that existed because of the number of times my life was spared, I couldn't do anything but cry out. "God, please get me out of this situation," I begged. I wanted to cry but knew I had to look and act as if everything was great. An hour went by, and a streetwalker, who was pregnant, was walking slowly down the street.

"Are you okay?" I asked as we walked past each other. The next thing I knew, she fell to the ground and started screaming. I stopped and started to call 9-1-1, but she begged me not to and said her baby was coming. I told her she needed to go to the hospital, but she still would not let me call for help. So instead, she gave birth on the street and cut her umbilical cord. She was going to walk away until some people walked up and called out to her. Then, she stopped and agreed to go to the hospital.

Shortly after, she left, and I was walking down the street when a car pulled up and wanted some service done. Without realizing what was happening, they drove me to a house where I was gang raped. I cried as I had never cried before. By now,

I wanted out and didn't care if that meant being killed. I just wanted out of the lifestyle I was trapped in. I curled up in a ball and cried out. "If there is a God and if He is real, please make a way for me to get out, and I promise I will serve you."

The next day when I was finally able to leave the house. I went to a truck stop knowing there would be a very low chance of being questioned. I connected with a truck driver because I was desperate to get out of L.A.

"Where are you headed? I asked.

He was going to Texas, and after looking at me and seeing some bruises on my arm and neck, he agreed to take me all the way back to Atlanta. This man was different from the truck drivers I had done business with before. The truck was clean, and there was no smell of drugs or cigarette smoke. Never once did he try to touch me while riding with him. Instead, he made me feel safe for the first time. About four days later, he dropped me off at a local hospital.

When I got out of the truck, I started throwing up, became dizzy, and fainted on the hospital emergency room floor. When I woke up, police officers, doctors, nurses, and others surrounded me.

"Can you hear me? one of them asked.

"Yes," I finally responded, confused about what was happening and where I was.

"What is your name? How did you get to the hospital? Do you know where you are?" they continued, peppering me with more questions.

"Jean Davis," I responded, answering their first question before they interrupted to ask me about my bruises.

"I'm good, and I just want to leave," I responded, ignoring the rest of their questions

"You can't leave because you're pregnant," the nurse told me.

"That is impossible," I stammered, wondering when the insanity in my life would end.

That night the hospital staff introduced me to some women that helped people who were being abused and scared for their lives find a safe place to live and start a better life. I looked at these women, took a deep breath, and said, "Okay, if this is a way to start new, I'm for it." After I went to a domestic shelter, a few weeks went by. During that time, the shelter staff began telling me about a place called the Pregnancy Resource Center, or PRC for short. I will never forget them asking me if I had a problem with the PRC being a "faith-based" center.

"What does that mean?" I asked.

"The people there believe in Jesus Christ," was their simple reply.

I laughed, smiled a little, and said, "No, that would be no bother to me."

The women said in the morning they would call the PRC and see if I could meet with one of the workers there. After speaking with the staff, I was nervous but thanked them and rolled over. Once I went to bed that night and thought about my conversation with them, I knew there was no other option.

"Okay, if this is a way to start new, I'm for it."

Right before I closed my eyes, I said, "Okay, God, if this is the way you are going to get me out, I'm all in." The doubt and lies were running through my mind. Questions of if this was going to work? Can they really help me? Was I crazy to make the statement in my heart that I was all in, no matter what it took? After fighting through the lies and doubts, I was determined to not just try to see if this would work but put every effort into making my life different.

When you think of bondage, what comes to mind? What does bondage mean or being bound mean? The dictionary gives the word a variety of meanings, ranging from captivity, being controlled by someone (slavery) or something (addiction, bondage to drugs), tied up, being under obligation (as in bound to a promise), and much more. When you are bound, you become hostage to a life you wish you could escape, whether good or bad.

Every person creates bondages all the time. For example, working, shopping, gambling, pornography, etc. The yoke of slavery is intertwined with false narratives that bondage is okay. Otherwise, you would never have been in whatever lifestyle keeps you bound. Have you ever felt you are stuck, imprisoned, locked into something? Living behind smoke screens because you didn't want to see it, believe it, or accept the reality that this was not what real life looks like? That is, if we can call our world "real life." That was what I was engaged in: bondage to the darkness of a life without freedom.

When I think of the bondage I lived in for almost all my life, I think of the Israelites when they were slaves to the Egyptians. When you read in the book of Exodus about the lives the Israelites lived, that was my life until Jesus heard my cry and made a way out.

The biblical story begins in Genesis 37 through 50 with Joseph, who was second in command to Pharaoh. When you come to Exodus, Joseph's family is living in Egypt. Joseph has passed away, and so has the Pharaoh, who knew what Joseph did for Egypt. Now, there is a new Pharaoh who does not like the Israelites. So, he assigns taskmasters over the people of Israel to build structures for the Egyptians. During the 400 years they lived in Egypt, the Israelites had to deal with their babies being murdered, beaten, whipped, and doing physically impossible things. There was no way out but death. Doesn't that sound like "The Game?"

So often, I could not physically do what men were asking me to do, or I would have someone pull a knife or gun on me. Every day, my body was used only to be their piece of merchandise that could be sold to the highest bidder, and I was in bondage to that life that found me doing things that I wish I could forget. Not realizing there is a God named Jesus Christ that gives us a way out of our sins. Still, since I did not know who God was, it was only by using drugs that I could escape from the nightmare.

The Israelites cried for 400 years to be saved, and for almost 30 years, I did the same. I did not realize I was calling on Jesus for help whenever a man hit me, raped me, or used my body for whatever they felt was good. Because we are sinners living in a fallen world, I never once felt as if God was allowing suffering to happen in my life. But there comes a day when Jesus does answer your cries for help.

The question is, are you going to answer Jesus when He comes for you? That is what I had to do. Jesus never answers your cry the way you think or want Him to. For the Jews, Jesus sent Moses and Aaron to speak and be the hands extended to God, giving them a chance to have hope. The chance to be set free from the bondage of darkness. The opportunity to truly experience a life of freedom.

When it feels like everything you have lived and decided in your life leads to pain and suffering, you long to experience grace and mercy. It was important for me to know what true love looked like, and I was beginning to have people cross my path who demonstrated that selfless love. I didn't trust it entirely in recognizing this love as what I was looking for. But, no matter what I felt, I knew this was what I had been looking for all my life.

That led to one moment in time that changed my whole life.

CHAPTER 21

THE PRC

I walked into an office I had passed by many times for a month. I sensed this place was my last hope, my final lifeline, and if I could somehow get in there, I would not fake trying to get help but accept the help this time. I just knew my life would change for the better than I could ever imagine.

I had just left an Alcoholics Anonymous meeting where people were using heroin in the bathroom and talking about using heroin after the meeting was over. One guy asked if I wanted to come with him to a house party while I was walking back to the shelter to do some heroin. I was about five months pregnant and trying not to use meth and definitely not heroin or drink alcohol. So, I told the guy no and continued to walk back to the domestic shelter.

"Are you going to start collecting items for your baby?" the shelter Program Manager, Theresa asked me when I returned in the afternoon.

"Sure," I replied, not wanting to engage with her on baby items because I was thinking of aborting the baby. So, I went down to the basement, where they stored clothes and different items. I didn't see anything I wanted at the time. After an hour or so, Theresa, called me back to the office.

"Did you find anything?"

"No, there was nothing I saw that I wanted."

"I will call a place I know that can help you get things for the baby," she replied.

"Okay," I said reluctantly.

A few minutes later, Theresa picked up the phone and began talking to another lady, then hung up.

"If you hurry, the lady I spoke to can see you today," she told me, scribbling down the address and telling me the name of the place.

"Okay," I said, glancing at the address and realizing it was just down the street from where the shelter was. So, I took the address and started walking. When I got there, I realized it was the same place I was hoping to get into. So many times, I had gone to the door, but it was locked and dark inside.

The place was called The Pregnancy Resource Center. When I stepped to the door and put my hand on the doorknob, something inside me said, *You are safe now. Everything is going to be okay. You don't have to run anymore, be hard, or act tough.* So, I opened the door, walked up the stairs, and opened another door to an office.

"How can I help you?" the woman there asked me.

"Theresa from the Domestic Violence shelter called, and I'm supposed to meet someone here," I told her.

"Oh, yes, she is expecting you. Wait here for a moment."

I was shaking, confused and unclear about why I was there. But I snapped out of my fog when a striking woman came around the corner. She was dressed in a skirt and blouse with black heels. She looked so happy, confident, and peaceful, something I only dreamed about having for myself.

"Hello," she said, introducing herself as Phyllis, but I paid no attention to her name. However, there was something about her that enchanted me. So, I followed her into the office that had a desk against one wall and a comfortable chair next to it.

"Please have a seat," she said, asking me my name and how she could help me.

At that moment, I let out a deep breath and started crying.

"I'm so tired," I sobbed and began telling this total stranger my story. Then, I surprised myself with what I said next.

"I want what you have," I told her, not even sure what I meant.

"I can't give that to you," she replied, "but I know a man named Jesus who can."

"Sure, why not?" I replied, not really knowing what this meant. *I had given every man in the world a chance, so why not give this man named Jesus a try,* I thought.

She then put her hands out, and I placed my hands in hers. As soon as we touched, a warm feeling came over my body. At that moment, I didn't want to smoke cigarettes or do any crystal meth. I just wanted what she had.

As soon as we touched, a warm feeling came over my body.

After Phyllis asked me if I knew a man named Jesus, she shared with me the salvation message found in Romans 10:9 and 10. "That if thou shalt confess with thy mouth the Lord Jesus, and shalt believe in thine heart that God hath raised him from the dead, thou shalt be saved. For with the heart man believeth unto righteousness, and with the mouth confession is made unto salvation." (KJV)

After I embraced the message and prayed the sinner's prayer for salvation, Phyllis asked about the baby.

"I don't want it."

We talked further, and I wavered.

"If it's a boy, I will keep it, but if it's a girl, I want to have an abortion," I said.

"Wait, just a second," she replied, rising from her chair to go into another room.

"We can do an ultrasound to check to see if the baby is healthy and okay," she told me when she returned.

"Okay," I said, following Phyllis into the second room, where a nurse was waiting to perform the ultrasound.

"It's a boy," the nurse told me when they returned a few minutes later.

"Okay, now what? I'm homeless and have no place to go."

The next few minutes began a journey that changed my life forever. And it all started with that meeting in the office of Phyllis Phelps and accepting Jesus Christ into my life.

I was just like the woman of Samaria Jesus encountered at the well. After all those years of being with different men and not feeling wanted, she didn't know what this day held, but Jesus did.

That day in the blazing hot desert sun with no shade and journeying for so long, we read:

> *"Now Jacob's well was there. Jesus therefore, being wearied from His journey, sat thus by the well. It was about the sixth hour. A woman of Samaria came to draw water. Jesus said to her, 'Give Me a drink.' For His disciples had gone away into the city to buy food." (John 4:6-8, NKJV)*

This passage tells us that Jesus was waiting for the woman to come to the well and knew who she was when He asked her for a drink of water. Like her, Jesus did the same thing when I went to Pregnancy Resource Center. He knew I was going to meet with her. He knew I was tired of the life I had been living. Mine was a life of searching for love and acceptance that only Jesus could fill, as He did with the woman at the well. The story continues:

> *"Jesus answered and said to her, 'Whoever drinks of this water will thirst again, but whoever drinks of the water that I shall give him will never thirst. But the water that I shall give him will become in him*

> *a fountain of water springing up into everlasting life.'"* (John 4:13-14, NKJV)

I was a person dead inside. The only thing I wanted to do was not to live anymore. I didn't want to have my unborn child because I was scared that they would be caught up in the life of violence, abuse, and jealousy I had known as normal. But Phyllis challenged me about embracing Jesus.

"And I'm not just talking about the Jesus we hear about," she said. "But do you personally know this man named Jesus Christ to where you know that when you call upon Him, He will answer your prayer?"

Before Jesus brought the plagues to the Egyptians and their land, look at what Jesus said to Moses in Exodus 6:6:

> *"Wherefore say unto the children of Israel, I am the Lord, and I will bring you out from under the burdens of the Egyptians, and I will rid you out of their bondage, and I will redeem you with a stretched out arm, and with great judgments."* (KJV)

Jesus Christ is in the business of delivering souls, setting the captive free, and leaving the ninety-nine for the one. When you read how Yahweh shows Himself, you realize people know God is the one fighting the battle. He is fulfilling His promise of saving His people, just like He fought and made a way to save me from the world of death and abandonment. But, just like the Jews had to walk across the Red Sea and out of Egypt, the same was true for me. I had to renounce Satan and his wicked ways. I not only believed the message of salvation, but I had hope that in trusting God, I would have a life of freedom.

But, just like everything in my life, I still questioned it. First, I had to decide if I would change my life. Then, I had to choose whom I was going to serve that day. If I was going to serve Jesus, which means a life of freedom, or if I was going to serve Satan, which means darkness and death. When I said the salvation prayer, I was to the point of death, and I wanted what Phyllis had: life, happiness, and hope that life would be better than it was.

So, my journey started in 2014 when I began attending a program for women needing help for addiction, abuse, and other issues.

CHAPTER 22

ESTHER

I will never forget the day I gave my life to Christ. When I looked into Phyllis' eyes, I knew my life would never be the same. When she put her hands out, welcoming me to take them as if to say, "come to a place that is loving, warm, and safe. A place where you don't have to be hard, pretend, or be scared to die."

The minute I touched Phyllis' hands, I felt something I had never felt before. The warmest feeling fell over me that wrapped around me like a cocoon. *I feel like I am breathing for the first time,* I thought at that moment. It was as if every pain I had inflicted on myself and others inflicted on me was gone.

I looked at Phyllis after I took her hands, and she asked what it felt like.

"I'm tired," was the only thing I could say at that moment. It was the first time someone asked me how I felt where I was comfortable telling the truth. She was not motivated to hurt me. I felt so safe at that moment while repeating the prayer for salvation. The warm feeling over my body removed any desire for smoking crystal meth, prostituting, or wanting to die. At that very second, I felt like someone truly loved me and could see me through all the pain.

Looking back over these past eight years, I can see that I was done with the life I was living and was desperate for something different. I was willing to try anything to pull myself out of death and the pain of abandonment. Jesus used Phyllis to reach me when no one else could. Of course, I had to be willing to receive what Phyllis was sharing about the gift Christ offered to me by dying on the cross. But Phyllis had to be willing to answer the call to share who Jesus Christ is and His ability to set me free from the world's abuse.

I think of how Esther was called for such a time to set the Jews free. She was chosen to be in the palace but didn't know when she became the queen, her people would be threatened with death. And, just like anyone called by God to fulfill a mission, we don't think we are capable or qualified to do what God asks us to do. But Jesus does not call the equipped. Jesus equips the called.

That is what Esther's uncle Mordecai said in Esther 4:14:

> *"For if thou altogether holdest thy peace at this time, then shall their enlargement and deliverance arise to the Jews from another place; but thou*

and thy father's house shall be destroyed: and who knoweth whether thou art come to the kingdom for such a time as this?" (KJV)

Esther was willing to walk by faith and not by sight when she went before the King of Persia to defend her people, the Jews. God used her not only to speak of her faith but to save the nation of Israel from destruction. The same way Christ used Phyllis to share her faith in who Jesus Christ is with me and save an unborn life. I walked into an office thinking I was going to have an abortion, even though everything in me knew that if I were to do so, I would walk back into death. But deep down, I hoped something would interrupt my path so I would not turn back to "The Game."

At that very second, I felt
like someone truly loved me.

That is why I can say that Phyllis was like Esther at that moment. For such a time in my life, Jesus used Phyllis to speak life to me.

At that moment, Jesus actually did what Psalm 40:1 says:

"I waited patiently for the Lord, and he inclined unto me, and heard my cry. He brought me up also out of an horrible pit, out of the miry clay, set my feet upon a rock, and established my goings." (KJV)

Jesus not only brought me out of the horrible pit, but He also snatched me from death's door. That cool fall day in October was the last time I would be a walking dead person, physically or spiritually. But, just like anything, when you stop doing something or want to change, there are always obstacles you must overcome.

For me, I had to fight for my freedom. Once I left the PRC and returned to the domestic shelter the next day, I woke up to people drinking beer and lying about me to the point that I packed my stuff into two duffle bags. But now I was homeless on the streets again and seven months pregnant with nowhere to go because I had to wait to enter the 18- to 24-month program. So, I walked to the PRC and called Phyllis.

"I had to leave the shelter and need help," I sobbed over the phone. That was the first time in my life that I had to decide if I would believe what Phyllis told me about this man named Jesus or go back to walking the streets, making money, and finding a way to leave the state. It was a life-changing decision.

CHAPTER 23

LEAVING "THE GAME"

Sitting on the steps at the PRC, I looked around and finally realized that I wanted something more from my life. I decided to stop running and fight for a life of freedom. I was done running and trying to survive another day. Now that I accepted that I was going to have a child, I needed to change my mindset of how to get by each day and life not being all about me. I had to start thinking about this new life I was carrying. *I vowed to myself that I would do whatever it took to give my child a better life than the one I had.*

I had gone through recovery programs before and lived in halfway houses, but this program was different. I could tell because Phyllis did not act or speak the way most women I had met over the years in state programs and halfway houses spoke or acted. Nevertheless, I was still determined to get the gift of salvation Phyllis had received. At the time, Phyllis didn't have her home for women up and running yet, so she brought me to the New Life Home for Women in Manchester, New Hampshire.

It was there that my thinking started to change. My mind became renewed, as it says in Romans 12:2. "And be not conformed to this world: but be ye transformed by the renewing of your mind, that ye may prove what is that good, and acceptable, and perfect, will of God." (KJV) While in the New Life program, I learned more about a man named Jesus. I learned he is a graceful, merciful, and trustworthy God who loves us so much that he sent Jesus to die for me and my sins. This gift included everything I had done to others and myself. The fact that he was still willing to die on the cross for me brought me to my knees. Over the time I was in the program, God showed me what He says will come to pass because He is not a man to lie. Jesus is truly the way, the truth, and the life.

I learned that to truly leave "The Game," I had to let go of my past and cling to Jesus. But, just like anything else, there is always pushback when you want to change or go in a different direction. Things in your past will remind you of what you were, along with thoughts that come into your mind saying, "You're not going to change," or "No one will believe you. Once a prostitute, always a prostitute."

It's like when you try to change the way you eat and see people eating ice cream, burritos, tacos, pasta, or whatever your favorite food is. You want to throw the towel in and give in to that temptation because it doesn't look bad for your health, but in reality, you're going back to eating the food that will kill you.

Proverbs 26:11 reminds us, "As a dog returneth to his vomit, so a fool returneth to his folly." (KJV) When you change your eating habits, you cannot see the changes other people see in you. That is until you step back and take a picture one day and see how much you have changed. Then, the rewards of change motivate you to keep going.

This was the same concept when I left "The Game." The longer I stayed out of that life and learned who Jesus was, the more I lost the desire to be in that life. What people don't understand is that when you say the salvation prayer to accept Jesus in your heart, it doesn't stop there. It's like wanting to get to know someone. You learn about all of their likes and dislikes. You understand what's in their heart and what kind of person they are. In the process, you start learning about yourself and seeing things you don't like. But that other person says, "Okay, I want to walk with you while you start working on yourself."

This is the difference between a person who says they are a Christian and a born-again believer. When you truly experience and encounter Jesus, you don't want the life you walked away from. Jesus says He is the bread of life and the living water and that you will never go thirsty again.

I had to let go of my past and cling to Jesus.

I can tell you when I got my taste of who Jesus really is, it echoed Psalm 34:8. "O taste and see that the Lord is good: blessed is the man that trusteth in him." (KJV) I wanted more of Him. The more I walked away from "The Game," the more I became disgusted by my old life. I felt like I couldn't get enough of Jesus. After graduating from the New Life program, I felt I was being called to Bible college. Once again, like anything new, the things people said to me made it scary to step out. As it says in Proverbs 18:21, "Death and life are in the power of the tongue: and they that love it shall eat the fruit thereof." (KJV)

Growing up, I was told that I would not amount to anything. They said I was stupid and would never graduate college because I could not read or write well. So, I was torn again. But this time, it was different. I was desperate for Jesus and all that He had for me. I had to try. I tried the New Life program and completed it, so why not try college? Over the next three years, I received a certificate and graduated with an associate degree in biblical theology. Once again, God showed me that living in "The Game" was keeping me helpless, without hope for a future, and nothing without my "daddy" or pimps.

But Jesus once again showed me that He truly is a man that cannot lie, and, as it says in John's gospel, you become free in Him. While Satan wants to steal, kill, and destroy, Jesus Christ comes to give you an abundant life. And if you are hungry to know Jesus, He does not leave you the way you were when you first met Him. And what if you aren't hungry to know this Jesus? What if you are just hungry to get out of your hell? You can just have the faith of a mustard seed that something will change if you reach out to Jesus.

Jesus wants to set you free from all the bondage of pain, guilt, shame, and regret. Jesus is not wanting to only change your outer appearance. Jesus wants to change you from the inside out with your heart being His focus. For me, that was scary because it meant I needed to no longer live in a victim mentality mode where people were out to get me, or things were happening to me because of my environment. Instead, I had to embrace the words of Revelation 12:11, "And they overcame him by the blood of the Lamb, and by the word of their testimony; and they loved not their lives unto the death." (KJV)

We are all a victim of something that we have experienced in life. The question that was asked of me was, "Am I going to stay in that victim mentality, or am I going to change so that I can help the next person come out of that life?" When you're in a victim state of mental and physical living, it is hard to help the next person because you still live as a victim, even though Jesus has set you free. After what was shared with me, I told myself, *No more will I allow my past to determine my future.*

But how do you go about not going back to your vomit? When have you never walked this life before? When every step you take is scary because the visions and voices of the past are still trying to haunt you?

CHAPTER 24

RUTH

When you have been beaten down by this world, you may come to a point in your life where you want something better. You become desperate for something you think will never happen for you.

When Phyllis told me about the New Life Home, it was so foreign to me, and I did not think it was true. *This doesn't work for women like me*, I thought, because I had been told by multiple shelters that they wouldn't take me. So, why would a Christian program take me if shelters would not? When you are kicked down to the point of just giving up, your window of opportunity starts to get smaller and smaller. But, when Phyllis looked into my eyes, I saw realness, truth, and the hope I was hanging on to, that is, the hope that this man named Jesus could help me. So, I became like Ruth.

You may ask, "Who is this woman in the Bible named Ruth?"

Ruth was a Moabite woman who grew up in a culture she knew wasn't right. The Moabites were a West-Semitic people who lived in the highlands east of the Dead Sea (now in west-central Jordan) and flourished in the ninth century B.C. Their ancestral founder was Moab, a son of Lot, a nephew of the Israelite patriarch Abraham. The Moabite religion practiced things that this nation does today. One of those Moabite beliefs was child sacrifice.

You can see that in 2 Kings 3:26-27:

> *"And when the king of Moab saw that the battle was too sore for him, he took with him seven hundred men that drew swords, to break through even unto the king of Edom: but they could not. Then he took his eldest son that should have reigned in his stead, and offered him for a burnt offering upon the wall. And there was great indignation against Israel: and they departed from him, and returned to their own land." (KJV)*

So, the Moabites had child sacrifice, which is the same as abortion that is practiced today in our nation. That was something I had to decide to walk away from and not harm my unborn child. But because Ruth was married to Naomi's son, an Israelite, she saw something different. The way that Naomi and her sons lived and believed was something Ruth wanted. As you read about Ruth, you will find that her husband died, but she still lived with Naomi, even though she could have returned home to her family at any point. Eventually, Naomi wanted to return home because not only did both of her sons die, but so did her husband.

When Naomi wanted to return, she had two daughters-in-law, Ruth and Orpah. Both had the choice if they wanted to walk away from a world they knew, understood, and survived in. What would you do if you had the chance to have your life changed? Would you go back to your life of depression, guilt, abandonment, abuse, hatred, manipulation, and believing things that are not natural or true? Or would you walk into the unknown, where you have been given a glimpse of hope, freedom, joy, and peace?

What would you do if you had the chance to have your life changed?

Everyone in this world has that option, no matter who you are or what your life looks like. You might think rich people have it all, yet see how rich people commit suicide, overdose, or die by gun violence. Then you have people who have gone to college and received degrees yet have an emptiness that can't be filled. The same for those who live in low-income situations and are barely surviving. That was what Ruth and Orpah were looking at. You could say they were at a fork in the road of their lives. Would they go back with Naomi to her country where the people, culture, and life differed from what they knew? Or would they return to the life they grew up with?

We continue reading Ruth 1 to find the answer.

> *"Then she [Naomi] arose with her daughters in law, that she might return from the country of Moab: for she had heard in the country of Moab how that the Lord had visited his people in giving them bread. Wherefore she went forth out of the place where she was, and her two daughters in law with her; and they went on the way to return unto the land of Judah. And Naomi said unto her two daughters in law, Go, return each to her mother's house: the Lord deal kindly with you, as ye have dealt with the dead, and with me. The Lord grant you that ye may find rest, each of you in the house of her husband. Then she kissed them; and they lifted up their voice, and wept. And they said unto her, Surely we will return with thee unto thy people. And Naomi said, Turn again, my daughters: why will ye go with me? are there yet any more sons in my womb, that they may be your husbands? Turn again, my daughters, go your way; for I am too old to have an husband. If I should say, I have hope, if I should have an husband also to night, and should also bear sons; Would ye tarry for them till they were grown? would ye stay for them from having husbands? nay, my daughters; for it grieveth me much for your sakes that the hand of the Lord is*

> *gone out against me. And they lifted up their voice, and wept again: and Orpah kissed her mother in law; but Ruth clave unto her. And she said, Behold, thy sister in law is gone back unto her people, and unto her gods: return thou after thy sister in law. And Ruth said, Intreat me not to leave thee, or to return from following after thee: for whither thou goest, I will go; and where thou lodgest, I will lodge: thy people shall be my people, and thy God my God: Where thou diest, will I die, and there will I be buried: the Lord do so to me, and more also, if ought but death part thee and me. When she saw that she was stedfastly minded to go with her, then she left speaking unto her. So they two went until they came to Bethlehem. And it came to pass, when they were come to Bethlehem, that all the city was moved about them, and they said, Is this Naomi?" (Ruth 1:6-19, KJV)*

Just like Ruth, I wanted what Phyllis had and would not leave her. So, when Phyllis brought me to New Life Home to drop me off, I trusted her. Not only did I trust her with my life but also with the life of my unborn son, whom I was carrying. When you read on in Ruth's story, which is only a total of four chapters, you will see that not only did she go back with Naomi to her land, but she listened to the wisdom of Naomi in how to do things.

At the end of the story, you find that Ruth became King David's great-grandmother and ultimately a part of Jesus Christ's lineage.

> *"Now Boaz went up to the gate and sat down there; and behold, the close relative of whom Boaz had spoken came by. So Boaz said, 'Come aside, friend, sit down here.' So he came aside and sat down. And he took ten men of the elders of the city, and said, 'Sit down here.' So they sat down. Then he said to the close relative, 'Naomi, who has come back from the country of Moab, sold the piece of land which belonged to our brother Elimelech. And I thought to inform you, saying, "Buy it back in the presence of the inhabitants and the elders of my people. If you will redeem it, redeem it; but if you will not redeem it, then tell me, that I may know; for there is no one but you to redeem it, and I am next after you.' And he said, 'I will redeem it.' Then Boaz said, 'On the day you buy the field from the hand of Naomi, you must also buy it from Ruth the Moabitess, the wife of the dead, to perpetuate the name of the dead through his inheritance.' And the close relative said, 'I cannot redeem it for myself, lest I ruin my own inheritance. You redeem my right of redemption for yourself, for I cannot redeem it.' Now this was the custom in former times in Israel concerning redeeming and exchanging, to confirm anything: one man took off his sandal and gave it*

to the other, and this was a confirmation in Israel. Therefore the close relative said to Boaz, 'Buy it for yourself.' So he took off his sandal. And Boaz said to the elders and all the people, 'You are witnesses this day that I have bought all that was Elimelech's, and all that was Chilion's and Mahlon's, from the hand of Naomi. Moreover, Ruth the Moabitess, the widow of Mahlon, I have acquired as my wife, to perpetuate the name of the dead through his inheritance, that the name of the dead may not be cut off from among his brethren and from his position at the gate. You are witnesses this day.' And all the people who were at the gate, and the elders, said, 'We are witnesses. The Lord make the woman who is coming to your house like Rachel and Leah, the two who built the house of Israel; and may you prosper in Ephrathah and be famous in Bethlehem. May your house be like the house of Perez, whom Tamar bore to Judah, because of the offspring which the Lord will give you from this young woman.' So Boaz took Ruth and she became his wife; and when he went in to her, the Lord gave her conception, and she bore a son. Then the women said to Naomi, 'Blessed be the Lord, who has not left you this day without a close relative; and may his name be famous in Israel! And may he be to you a restorer of life and a nourisher of your old age; for your daughter-in-law, who loves you, who is better to you than seven sons, has borne

> *him.' Then Naomi took the child and laid him on her bosom, and became a nurse to him. Also the neighbor women gave him a name, saying, 'There is a son born to Naomi.' And they called his name Obed. He is the father of Jesse, the father of David."*
> *(Ruth 4:1-17, NKJV)*

As Ruth did, I had to decide to follow Christ. It's not easy, and we are clueless like babies at the beginning of our walk with Him. Phyllis has been a mentor to me, as was Naomi to Ruth. God provides those to all His children giving people hope that there are people like Phyllis out there for them, and it doesn't always come fast or easy. But Phyllis showed me how to walk with Jesus, and there are great results when I do!

My whole life has completely changed. The bondage of generations has been broken!

CHAPTER 25

ENTERING A NEW LIFE

Everything was different when Ruth entered a new life with Naomi. It was the same for me. There were things I had to let go of if I wanted this new life Phyllis introduced me to. Just like everything else I started, it was easy. If you ask anyone trying to get clean from drugs or alcohol, the first thirty days are a breeze. Any government program I have been involved with only allows you to stay in the program for up to 90 days, and then you are back on the streets. So, for those ninety days, you are clean and doing okay. There were times I would last a couple of weeks or months before I would start using again and end up with a pimp. It is a vicious cycle I couldn't get out of.

The New Life program was completely different. Not only was it an 18-to-24 four-month program, but it also forced me to look at my life and deal with my reality. During this time, I had my second son, Noah, and had to learn to be a mother. Even though I had a son nine years earlier, I was not a real mother to him. I had to realize that, once again, I would be a single mother because I would never know who Noah's father was, and I still do not. I had to learn to forgive the people that hurt me physically, emotionally, mentally, and spiritually.

The time in the New Life program was challenging because I had to understand how I was living and brought up to live wasn't real life. I had to learn who Jean Davis is. Over time, I read the entire Bible to understand who Jesus Christ was (and is) and why He wanted to save me. After I read the Bible and saw how caring and loving Jesus was to me, I longed for more. I wanted to consume any teaching to learn more about Jesus and His Word. The more I studied the Bible, the more I could forgive the people who hurt me. I started learning to have confidence in myself and build standards based on the Bible. I began setting goals to build up my faith. Negative people in my life had said I would never graduate from college. Yet not only did I graduate from the New Life program, but I also received my Associate Degree in Biblical Studies.

Throughout my journey, I often wanted to give up, throw in the towel, and say, "This is not for me. Why did I start this?" But I tell you, the reward of fighting for your life is so worth it that you will not want to do anything else. There comes the point in life when you decide to fight for the freedom Jesus speaks about in John 8:36, when He says, "If the Son therefore shall make you free, ye shall be free indeed." (KJV)

The more I studied the Bible, the more I could forgive the people who hurt me.

So, every day in the New Life program, I fought for the freedom that Jesus wanted to give me. There were times in my journey when I had to denounce things I didn't even know I needed to be set free from, such as card reading, palm reading, and men I lived for to get approval. I had to reject the lies people told me over the years and do what 2 Corinthians 10:5 says. "Casting down imaginations, and every high thing that exalteth itself against the knowledge of God, and bringing into captivity every thought to the obedience of Christ." (KJV)

Once I did that, I looked to Ephesians 1:3-14, which says:

> *"Blessed be the God and Father of our Lord Jesus Christ, who hath blessed us with all spiritual blessings in heavenly places in Christ: According as he hath chosen us in him before the foundation of the world, that we should be holy and without blame before him in love: Having predestinated us unto the adoption of children by Jesus Christ to himself, according to the good pleasure of his will, To the praise of the glory of his grace, wherein he hath made us accepted in the beloved. In whom we have redemption through his blood, the forgiveness of sins, according to the riches of his grace; Wherein he hath abounded toward us in all wisdom and prudence; Having made known unto us the*

> *mystery of his will, according to his good pleasure which he hath purposed in himself: That in the dispensation of the fulness of times he might gather together in one all things in Christ, both which are in heaven, and which are on earth; even in him: In whom also we have obtained an inheritance, being predestinated according to the purpose of him who worketh all things after the counsel of his own will: That we should be to the praise of his glory, who first trusted in Christ. In whom ye also trusted, after that ye heard the word of truth, the gospel of your salvation: in whom also after that ye believed, ye were sealed with that holy Spirit of promise, which is the earnest of our inheritance until the redemption of the purchased possession, unto the praise of his glory." (KJV)*

In the beginning, it was not easy to change my thinking. Over time I started learning about grace through the examples I was shown in the program. Romans 12:2: "And be not conformed to this world: but be ye transformed by the renewing of your mind, that ye may prove what is that good, and acceptable, and perfect, will of God." (KJV)

You must want to change and say, "enough is enough," and let the words of Jesus wash over you to renew your mind. Then, sit back and watch how your life changes for the better.

CHAPTER 26

WALKING A NEW LIFE

After so many years of being beaten and torn down, I never thought I would be able to experience having grace shown to me. Let alone show myself grace after everything I had done to people and myself. "Can you see the grace that was shown by God to Jean?"

I asked myself that question while writing this book. After being in prostitution for almost 20 years, being freed by finding out who Christ is, and allowing Him to guide me out of the nightmare and darkness, I can only praise God.

Jesus showed me He is a gentleman who does not push me into giving up things. When I first came to Christ, I was adamant that I would never marry because of the life I had lived. Most women my age want to be swept off their feet by Taye

Diggs, Vin Diesel, or Dwayne Johnson. I wanted none of that. Why would I when for the last 20 years I had been threatened and told to lay on my back, often with a fist in my face?

It wasn't the only reason I didn't want to be married. The other reason was I was in so much pain while having sex. Can you imagine telling my husband, "No, I can't have sex because it is too painful to the point of tears?" Toward the end of my life in "The Game," I cried almost every time I had sex. So, for the past five years, I feared that if I were to be married, my husband would want to make love, and I would have to say no.

Then, one April day, I began having terrible pain before, during, and after my menstrual cycle. I decided to make a doctor's appointment to end my agony. When I went to the appointment, they asked me if they could run tests. I then had to wait for the results.

It had been about three weeks, and I had forgotten that I was supposed to get a phone call from my doctor's office. Then, one morning I was at work riding in my car with my co-worker to a meeting when my phone rang. I answered the call, and to my surprise, the nurse from my doctor's office said that my tests and ultrasound had come back. I had two tumor cysts on my ovaries. The nurse explained that my right ovary was as big as a tennis ball, and my left was as big as a baseball.

"You'll need to come in and have them checked to see if they are cancerous," she said matter-of-factly.

Jesus showed me He is a gentleman.

I had no words and started crying. For months after that phone call, I went in for different scans to see if what they were calling tumor cysts were still growing. Finally, the doctor determined it wasn't good that I was experiencing so much pain from the size of the cysts.

The decision was made for me to have surgery, but I would have to wait two more months. There were days I would cry, and sometimes it felt like I was in labor pains. Through the months, I had been praying and seeking God's wisdom about whether or not I should be ready to not have any more children. Unfortunately, I am a single mom who can't sit down with my husband for advice on this life-changing decision.

Meanwhile, my son Noah was constantly asking for a father and to be a big brother. So, I would tell him to ask God. I faced a major decision. Due to how big the tumors were, the doctors suggested I have a hysterectomy. But I had it in my spirit that I would have another baby and be married someday. So, I told the surgeon I did not want a hysterectomy, but if they could save my ovaries, that would be great.

Then one day, while praying, I felt in my spirit that my right ovary needed to go and that the left one was going to stay. So, the day finally arrived for me to have surgery, and the doctor came in.

"We'll do our best to save both your ovaries," she said, adding that the surgery would take two to three hours.

"Thank you, but it's okay if you need to take out my right one," I replied.

The next thing I remember is waking up screaming because I could not move my right arm. My shoulder got dislocated during the surgery and needed to be popped back into place.

When I got into the recovery room, I discovered that my surgery had complications. It ended up being five hours long. First, they removed my right ovary because the tumor covered up multiple cysts, some of which were close to my fallopian tube. Unfortunately, the cysts they were trying to remove were bleeding out. Then, after the doctors explained what had happened in the operating room, they started investigating how my shoulder got dislocated. When the results came back, they explained that somehow during surgery, my body got rolled on top of my arm, dislocating it.

Through the entire process, God showed me that there were more than the tumors He was fixing in my heart.

CHAPTER 27

ENJOYING FREEDOM

After my major surgery, I was able to look at myself differently. I no longer saw myself as fat or thought no man would want me. I no longer saw a woman who others in my old life called damaged goods. Instead, as I looked in the mirror, I saw a woman in love with Jesus for who He was and is. I was excited to be on the journey the Lord had me on.

I had my surgery in 2019, and COVID hit the nation the following year. It was a tough time because my passion is to save souls, and I desire to share the gospel of Jesus in any way I can, telling others how He has set me free. But because of COVID limiting work and being a single mother, I prayed for God to help me to support and take care of my son, Noah.

After I had been working, I finally landed a position at a hospital as an assistant in the Human Resources Department. At first, I did not understand why I was there because my degree was in biblical theology. However, in the New Life program and at my college, I learned that your ministry is where the Lord has you. So, I would share Jesus in any way I could and wherever he put me. Once the government came out with the COVID vaccine, I remember that the Hospital Association said to obtain a religious exemption, "You would have to prove your God." *Not a problem*, I thought, and during that time, I was able to help many people get an exemption.

But even though I was able to help people in little ways, I still was not satisfied. I wanted to be able to get women off the streets and help anyone desperate for change as I had been. So, from 2020 to August 2022, I worked in the hospital as an assistant, learning about how a company works, how to speak to people, and how to be a leader that people. It was not easy for me through this process, knowing I came from a world where people told me what to do and how to do it. Even though I was learning a lot, I still felt like I was missing something.

In August, my life changed forever. I felt called to fast for 40 days. What does fasting mean biblically? Fasting is giving up food for a period to focus your thoughts on God. While fasting, many people read the Bible, pray, or worship. Fasting is found throughout the Old and New Testaments of the Bible. During this period, I sought Jesus like I never had before. I wanted to be like Isaiah when he wrote, "I heard the voice of the Lord, saying: 'Whom shall I send, and who will go for Us?' Then said I, 'Here am I! Send me.'" (Isaiah 6:8, NKJV)

I did not care where Jesus wanted to send me. All I knew was that I wanted to do His will. I remember telling a general surgeon that he saved lives so that they could breathe another day. I wanted to help save souls so that they could live for eternity. Walking with Jesus these past eight years, my heart hurt for the lost and hurting people in this nation.

After I had fasted, I felt I was being led to work in a women's ministry. I had sensed for years that I was to work in ministry, but I didn't know what kind. So, I spoke to my pastor about what I felt, and he agreed that he could see me working in a ministry like that within a few years. Meanwhile, I continued working at my job and practicing what Colossians 3:17 says: "And whatsoever ye do in word or deed, do all in the name of the Lord Jesus, giving thanks to God and the Father by him." (KJV)

Everything changed on October 13, 2022. "I want to give up," I told God that morning while driving to work. "I don't want to work at the hospital anymore." I was so sad that I repeated what King David said in Psalm 43:5: "Why art thou cast down, O my soul? And why art thou disquieted within me? Hope in God: for I shall yet praise him, who is the health of my countenance, and my God." (KJV)

Later that day, I finished a spreadsheet audit and took a break. I looked down at my phone and saw that I had some unread emails, including one from my church. I opened it to see who needed prayer so I could pray for them. I was not expecting to read the words that followed. One of my church sisters told me her daughter had died from an overdose. I broke down and cried over her loss, weeping and thanking the Lord Jesus for saving me from the same fate. I wept because it meant another soul I could not share the gospel with.

"What's wrong?" several co-workers asked when they saw me crying. I told them, and they suggested I go see my director. So, I went into my director's office and told her what had happened. The words I heard next shocked me.

"You couldn't have saved her," she said.

"I couldn't save her, but I can save someone else," was my angry reply. "I'm not meant to be sitting behind two computer screens when people are dying," I added. While driving home after getting off work, I was listening to a sermon titled "Don't Quit." *Okay, God, I'm not giving up*, I prayed.

The next day I felt the need to go see Phyllis. "Come in," she warmly greeted me, handing me an application for a director's position at a Vermont pregnancy resource center. Phyllis thought of me because a month prior, we had prayed and asked for me to work in full-time ministry. I was not thinking of being an executive director. That was October 14, 2022, and for the next few days, I completed the application and got two letters of recommendation. During that time, I was also praying and worshiping, believing God for something great. The following Tuesday, the Holy Spirit put it on my heart to submit my resignation at the hospital. I stepped out on faith the same day I submitted my application at the PRC.

I was also praying and worshiping,
believing God for something great.

The many times the Lord has moved in my life, I had to walk by faith, embracing what Hebrews 11:1 says. "Now faith is the substance of things hoped for, the evidence of things not seen." (KJV) I had to walk by faith that Jesus had me. So, after submitting my application, I drove to my job, arriving at about 10:30. I already had a meeting scheduled with my manager and director to do my job review. However, they were still in a different meeting, so I took my time and wrote my resignation letter.

When their meeting was over, they asked if I was ready for our meeting. "Yes," I replied, shaking because I had never resigned from a job without already having another one lined up. It's all or nothing with the Lord because Jesus says either you are for Him or against Him. So, I stepped into that meeting, knowing what I needed to do.

After a few minutes of listening, I asked if I could give them something. "Yes," my manager replied as I handed her my resignation letter. She was speechless.

"Do you have a new job?" she asked.

"No," I replied honestly since I had just applied. My resignation letter gave the hospital a two-and-a-half-week notice. Once I handed them the letter, it became official, and the clock began ticking. After that, there was no going back.

By Thursday, I had not heard anything from the PRC, and my manager came to me and told me about a different position in the hospital that I might like, but it required doing a few tasks. As I was trying to do what she suggested, something inside me said, *Jesus brings things to you, and Satan makes you chase things.* So, I went outside and called the PRC to find out if the board president had seen my application. There had been no progress, so it was still a waiting game.

I think of Psalm 46:10: "Be still, and know that I am God: I will be exalted among the heathen, I will be exalted in the earth." (KJV) Shortly before 7:00 the next morning, the PRC president emailed me to set up an interview, asking if I was available the following Monday at 6:00 p.m.

"Yes," I eagerly replied, knowing Monday couldn't come fast enough. On Saturday, I panicked the entire day. All I could think about was how challenging the opportunity would be and whether I was qualified enough. Was I crazy because this was a huge step to becoming a director and taking on such a challenging opportunity? It was almost like a dream happening to someone else. However, by Sunday, I had calmed down and returned to the Isaiah mindset of, "Here am I, send me." He confirmed what I had heard him say during my 40-day fast, that I would lead a woman's ministry, and reassured me it was time for this to happen.

Finally, Monday evening arrived, and my interview lasted an hour and twenty minutes, and I thought I did well. Shortly after leaving, I received an email from the president saying they would like to move forward with me. I was thrilled to have passed their initial interview!

Understand I was still working at the hospital, telling people I got the job even though nothing was official. But I have learned that you must speak it as if it is so that it becomes so. A week went by. Nothing. I began getting nervous, even though I still believed God. Then on October 28, I got an email saying that the next meeting was scheduled for November 8. Now, understand that my last day at the hospital was November 4.

So, I'm facing the test of whether I will stay focused on Jesus and believe this of Him or rely on what I see in the physical. You constantly get tested to see if you are willing to go the whole way, or do you say, "I can't," because you see what is around you? So, while waiting for the second meeting, I had to remind myself that Jesus is my provider and that He has been with me every step of the way. He will never leave me nor forsake me. During the entire time of waiting, the Lord reminded me every single day that He called me to this position by having people like my pastor and others say, "Yes," I am the right person for this position. I knew in my heart that this would bring me full circle from where I started my walk with the Lord eight years earlier.

Finally, November 8 came, and I arrived for my second interview. After I left, I was not entirely confident that the board would want me, so I started becoming discouraged again. I received an email a few hours later asking me when a good time would be to call. The next day, I received a call from the board president offering me the position of Executive Director of the Pregnancy Resource Center. Not only did God show me that His Word does not come back void, but that He is not a man that will lie.

I am thrilled with this new position. I can now be free in a new way. Not only am I free from drugs and prostitution, but I am free to worship and do what I love. I feel like the woman at the well who went to her town and shared how Jesus knew everything about her and set her free. I can now do the same thing!

To have genuine faith means you must have absolute trust. And over the years, Jesus has shown me how to trust Him. I have learned that Jesus only wants a relationship with me, and I honestly can say that I love my God, Jesus. Not for what He has blessed me with but for the fact that He loved me when no one else did and has shown me mercy and grace when I did not deserve it. That is why I hold no condemnation for myself because Jesus does not.

CHAPTER 28

NO MORE CONDEMNATION

No more condemnation. I think of that when I read the Bible passage about the woman caught in adultery.

> *"Then the scribes and Pharisees brought to Him a woman caught in adultery. And when they had set her in the midst, they said to Him, 'Teacher, this woman was caught in adultery, in the very act. Now Moses, in the law, commanded us that such should be stoned. But what do You say?' This they said, testing Him, that they might have something of which to accuse Him. But Jesus stooped down and wrote on the ground with His finger, as though*

> *He did not hear. So when they continued asking Him, He raised Himself up and said to them, 'He who is without sin among you, let him throw a stone at her first.' And again He stooped down and wrote on the ground. Then those who heard it, being convicted by their conscience, went out one by one, beginning with the oldest even to the last. And Jesus was left alone, and the woman standing in the midst. When Jesus had raised Himself up and saw no one but the woman, He said to her, 'Woman, where are those accusers of yours? Has no one condemned you?' She said, 'No one, Lord.' And Jesus said to her, 'Neither do I condemn you; go and sin no more.'" (John 8:3-11, NKJV)*

When Jesus told the woman, "Sin no more," this was the same thing He told me when He came into my life. He gave me hope that I would be a wife to a man who loved God and me. Also, Christ telling me to sin no more didn't feel like a mandate. Instead, I was learning a new level of grace and could now show grace even to people who had hurt me to the core of my being. I no longer had to worry about men condemning me for whatever sounded good to them.

I now have this joy that won't let go. I looked into His eyes, and He freed my soul; my soul knows it. Through all of the pain for my ovaries, being a single mother, and the life I left behind, I still had the question of what woman would want to be with a man knowing that it would be painful to make love with them if they were married. That is what I thought until God whispered to my heart that I would be married one day.

The other scripture God laid on my heart was in Matthew 17:20, where Jesus says if we have faith as small as a mustard seed, we can move mountains. That is exactly what God did when I had the surgery. It relieved the pain and gave me hope that God would fulfill His promise to me.

God continues to work through me on grace. He showed in my position in the hospital why I can't show grace to people even though God has shown me the most grace ever by dying on the cross so that my sins could be forgiven. There was a deep root in me that I had buried but did not get rid of. That root was the fact that men that I dealt with in my life never showed me grace. These men did not care if I was bleeding, in pain, or screaming. Money had to be made. Even though I was grateful that Christ saved me, I was not showing the true Gospel of grace to the same type of women coming out of the similar lifestyle God saved me from. The grace shown to me had to be given to them. Instead, the root that was buried deep in my soul was bitterness and hatred.

Because you have read this far, you can see why I would have a hard time in this area of my life. But Scripture warns about letting a root of bitterness spring up and cause trouble, warning that many become defiled because of it. Anger and jealousy spring up out of bitterness. And, when God showed me this root of bitterness in my life, I cried because I love and feel empathy for the women trying to come out of being human trafficked.

So, I prayed to overcome this nasty root within me. After praying and fasting, the Lord showed me that I needed to feel pity for the men that hurt me emotionally and physically. He loves them and wants everyone to be saved and not perish. I don't know why those men did those things to me, but I needed to forgive them just like Christ forgave me at Calvary. Yes, it is hard to forgive people who may have hurt you in more ways than one, but that is what the cross is for. Christ washed His blood over us when we came to Him, and He forgives our sins as far as the east is from the west. (Psalm 103:12)

After reading about my journey through the tortures and triumphs of life done to me, I can understand that you may not feel this story applies to you. But I can tell you it does. I can say that because, at the end of the day, I was just surviving.

Some of you right now are living paycheck to paycheck. You may be a single parent trying to raise your children or a child in this world who feels as though they do not care about right or wrong. Maybe you have an alcohol or other life-controlling issue you can't overcome. Every way you turn, it seems like two steps forward but four steps back. That was my life. Every way I looked, I was going deeper and deeper into a black hole with only two possible outcomes: death or jail. All because I was surviving day by day.

I prayed to overcome this nasty root within me.

I am here to tell you that you no longer must just survive. After everything I had done, when I finally came to the end of myself with little strength left, I called out to Jesus. "I waited patiently for the Lord; And He inclined to me, and heard my cry. He also brought me up out of a horrible pit, Out of the miry clay, And set my feet upon a rock, And established my steps." (Psalm 40:1-2, NKJV) That sounds great, right? But is it true?

The first thing I did after calling on the name of Jesus was to find someone who could help me get to the point where I could believe that God was really going to establish my steps. The same thing can happen to you. If you want a change in your life and believe that God can change you as He has done for me, then acknowledge this aloud:

> *"But what does it say? 'The word is near you, in your mouth and in your heart' (that is, the word of faith which we preach): that if you confess with your mouth the Lord Jesus and believe in your heart that God has raised Him from the dead, you will be saved. For with the heart one believes unto righteousness, and with the mouth confession is made unto salvation. For the Scripture says, 'Whoever believes on Him will not be put to shame.' For there is no distinction between Jew and Greek, for the same Lord over all is rich to all who call upon Him. For 'whoever calls on the name of the Lord shall be saved.'"* (Romans 10:8-13, NKJV)

AMEN! AMEN!

> *"Finally, there is laid up for me the crown of righteousness, which the Lord, the righteous Judge,*

> *will give to me on that Day, and not to me only but also to all who have loved His appearing." (2 Timothy 4:8, NKJV)*

I believe the Lord pressed these scriptures on my heart for anyone reading this book. Yes, we all do things that are not right because we are sinners. However, we need to understand that the God we serve sent His son to die on the cross so we may have an opportunity to receive the Crown of Righteousness. I had bad experiences with men in my life. Others may have a past the same as mine or worse. But I am still learning that God is a merciful and gracious God who sees who we are under the blood of the cross. In other words, if we strive to be like Christ in our everyday walk by staying close to a church family, praying, seeking God, and continually wanting to be renewed in our minds, the closer I believe we will be to receiving the Crown of Righteousness that Christ has for us when we see Him again.

Throughout my time writing this book, the Lord Jesus repeatedly reminded me that He is my confidence. No longer do I have that bitterness of hatred and anger in me. No longer is there fear of how I am going to please man. The bitterness and need to please people had such a death grip on me that I allowed Satan to use it to control me. To look for a love that was never real set me down a dark and deadly path. Now every day, God gives me something to rejoice about and be in love with.

If you think after writing about my pain and hurts that I do not have any more issues, then you must not know much about being a sinner. The Bible says in Romans 3:23, "For all have sinned and fall short of the glory of God." (NKJV) Do I still have things that I need to work on? Yes, but the deep roots in me when I was writing this book are not deep anymore, to the point that God has removed them. I believe more than ever when Jeremiah said this that it was true then and is now. "It is of the Lord's mercies that we are not consumed, because his compassions fail not. They are new every morning: great is thy faithfulness." (Lamentations 3:22-23, KJV)

I have been a born-again Christian for more than eight years, and the love that Christ has shown me no man on earth can ever match. I am no longer living to please or win a man's heart. The heart I have already won over is the Creator of heaven and earth. God is so pleased with me that He has told me since day one, "You will be a crown of splendor in the Lord's hand, a royal diadem in the hand of your God. No longer will they call you Deserted, or name your land Desolate." (Isaiah 62:3-4, NIV)

I am alive in Him. No more being ashamed of my past. Since Christ walked on the road to Calvary and died for my sins, I do not have to be in a desolate land. God has promised me that I am covered under the blood that His son shed for me. For that reason, I continue to do as Proverbs 3:5-6 declares. "Trust in the Lord with all thine heart; and lean not unto thine own understanding. In all thy ways acknowledge him, and he shall direct thy paths." (KJV)

I pray that after reading this book, God has stirred up within you a desire to change and want to get to truly know who Jesus Christ really is. If you or someone you know needs help or knows someone that needs help in changing from surviving to living, please reach out to a local Bible-believing church or ministry that focuses on these things. Don't give up on wanting a different life God has for you.

No longer do I have that bitterness of hatred and anger in me.

Christ wants to help you become free from a life of death so that you can see the glory of who He really is. He is "a father to the fatherless, a defender of widows, is God in his holy dwelling." (Psalm 68:5, NIV) He protects you no matter the valleys or if you are on the high mountaintops. "For God so loved the world that he gave his one and only Son, that whoever believes in him shall not perish but have eternal life." (John 3:16, NIV)

I am learning that we must be willing to surrender the hurt and pain of the roots that are holding us bound in chains. We become free in Christ when saying, "If anyone desires to come after Me, let him deny himself, and take up his cross, and follow Me." (Matthew 16:24, NKJV) "Do not be afraid or terrified because of them, for the Lord your God goes with you; he will never leave you nor forsake you." (Deuteronomy 31:6, NIV)

I can attest to that in my own life. Since I left "The Game," I have finished college with an AA degree, graduated from a program for women with children, and am back on my feet as a productive member of society. I can work with women who come from similar backgrounds and show them that there is a better way. "'For I know the plans I have for you,' declares the

Lord, 'plans to prosper you and not to harm you, plans to give you hope and a future.'" (Jeremiah 29:11, NIV)

Now, every day I wake up knowing that God has a future and plans for me. I no longer have to wake up every morning worried about having enough money to pay for the hotel. Because I decided to follow Christ, I can break free from the handcuffs of this world.

I pray and hope this story touched you in some way to let you know that you're not alone. I hope you will seek what God has for you in His kingdom. As Christ says in James 4:8, "Come near to God and he will come near to you. Wash your hands, you sinners, and purify your hearts, you double-minded." (NIV) God will never look at you like your land is deserted. Instead, he will make you fruitful and give you living water so that it will overflow in your life, your family's life, and everyone around you.

May God bless and cover you in the path He has laid before you.

With Love,

Jean Davis

ABOUT THE AUTHOR

Jean Davis is an overcomer of human trafficking. After almost 20 years trapped in "The Game" and the fear of and threat of rape, violation, and drug addiction, Jesus Christ snatched her from death's door and brought her to freedom. Her story is one of God's grace, freedom from prostitution, and healing from years of abuse. The mother of two children, Jean has graduate from a program for abused women and gone on to earn an associate degree in biblical theology. She now serves as the Executive Director of one of the Pregnancy Resource Centers in Vermont.